SICK DAYS

by Chloe Alessandra Henkel

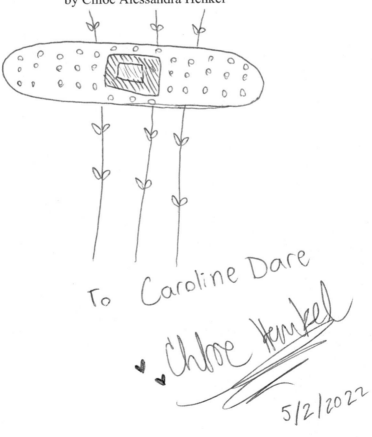

To Caroline Dare

Chloe Henkel

5/2/2022

This book, as well as the words and images within it and on its cover are Copyright © 2022 by Chloe Henkel and may not be reproduced without permission. Thank you!

To all of my beautiful fireflies: please keep glowing, no matter how dark it gets.

It's nighttime where I am right now. And I'm a little bit in love with it: with the way the stars are, and with the soft glow of the lamps scattered across my room.

Sure, sometimes I end up staying up because my thoughts are spiraling in my veins are made of carbonation and firecrackers but
                      a lot of times I stay up because I love it.
                      I love the way that no one can really expect anything of you when you're alone in your room at night. That no one can justify asking how you spent your one-to-two-a.m., that there's no where to go, unless you decide to go somewhere, and everywhere you do choose to go is a choice that feels like an adventure.

What I mean to say is that I love the night because, like so many things, I used to let it swallow me
but now
I've made it
my own.

Sections

-Trigger Warning (pg. 9)

-Author's Note (pg. 11)

-In the Doctor's Waiting Room (pg. 13)
an introduction

-I've Felt These Things and Survived (pg. 21)
the heavy section, where we talk about the darkness

-Your Next Birthday (pg. 170)
the section to skip ahead to if you need cheering up

-(Not) The End (pg. 255)
a conclusion of sorts

-Resources (pg. 258)

- Things to Do When Struggling (pg. 261)

-About the Author (pg. 272)

TRIGGER WARNING

This book talks about triggering topics, including:

-Mental Illness (anxiety, depression, OCD, etc.)

-BFRBs (Body-focused repetitive behaviors)

-Self-harm

-Suicidal Thoughts

and more.

I did my best to put more detailed trigger-warnings before particularly triggering pieces, or those that deal with a very specific trigger, but please exercise self-care before, during, and after deciding if you want to continue reading.

If you feel stressed, triggered, or are struggling at any point, please reach out to the mental health resources listed on page 258.

Author's Note

Before you jump into the book, there are some things I'd like to clarify! Although I do talk about mental disorders and mental health issues in this book, I am not a therapist or a mental health professional. I am a writer, speaking from my own experiences. This book isn't intended to diagnose or treat any mental health condition: please, please, please reach out to a therapist, or to other mental health resources if you're struggling, and/or think you might have any of the disorders mentioned in this book.

Additionally, because this might be a bit confusing for some people: in this book, I talk about experiencing anxiety, panic attacks, depressive episodes, suicidal thoughts, self-harm, trichotillomania, OCD, and other things. These are *not* all the result of the same disorder: I just happen to have struggled with all of them. Many, many people struggling with trichotillomania (or other BFRBs) don't self-harm, have depression, feel suicidal, or experience any of the other issues mentioned. Their only disorder/symptom may be hair-pulling. Similarly, most people with anxiety disorders or clinical depression don't develop trichotillomania. And so on, and so forth. Then, of course, many others do struggle with more than one of these issues, or others not mentioned.

My point is this: I do not want this book to increase confusion or stigma around any of these disorders. If you're interested in learning more about a specific disorder, please speak to a mental health professional, or research it using reliable health resources, as opposed to jumping to conclusions based just on my portrayal of my own experiences.

With all that said, I really hope you enjoy the book!

IN THE DOCTOR'S WAITING ROOM

If you're struggling, please reach out ; (Further resources listed on pg. 258)

Sick Days

I am so proud of you for fighting your fight.
For staying afloat.
For coming back up after you sink,
pulled under by sharks with fangs
that nobody else seems to catch
more than a brief glimpse of
through the choppy waves.

It's the definition of injustice that you have to
to fight, to falter, to bite bullets until your teeth buckle
but I am frighteningly proud of you
for pulling through
all this pain.

I hope you know I mean it.
I hope you know that I'd give anything
to hug you right now
unless you don't like hugs,
in which case
I'd give anything to give you whatever it is
that lets you know you're loved
and I hope you'll hug, hold, love
yourself in my place.

Because you, my darling,
are perfect.

You, my friend,
mean everything.

Crisis Textline ; *CrisisTextline.org* ; Text # 741741 (in US and Canada)

Chloe Alessandra Henkel

What are you in here for anyway?
I mean, obviously you picked up this book
for some reason.
Right?

Okay, I'm sorry.
That was too forward.
I just mean that
if you want to tell me
what's going on in that mind of yours,
I'll listen.
And if you want someone to keep you company
in this waiting room
or to go into your doctor's appointment
with you,
well,
I'd follow you
all the way to the moon and back.

My point is this:
from this point forward,
you're anything but
alone.

If you're struggling, please reach out ; (Further resources listed on pg. 258)

Sick Days

To me, poetry feels a lot like rambling.
I don't know if this is because that's really how it's done or
because I'm a bad poet
but I suppose it's a little late to try and tell the difference.
I was born with two holes in my heart:
I don't even remember what it felt like,
but it sounds so poetic
if you forget the goriness and logistical aspects of it.
So anyway, I was born with holes in my heart.
The doctors cut me open
sewed me up
said they'd fixed me
and sent my parents' insurance
a bill bigger than my net worth.
But the truth is,
I think they were liars
because as long as I can remember I've been
trying to re-fill myself.
Feeling a little too light or
a little too hollow
and my heart has always been
slightly off-center in my chest and I
can't help but wonder if they fixed it at all
because maybe—just maybe—
they didn't.
And maybe
just maybe
that's why I am the way that I am:
all jagged lines and red-rimmed eyes
with no clear plans to-date.
To me, poetry feels a lot like rambling
and rambling feels a lot like a steady stream of water
re-filling all the cracks, cervices, and off-kilter places
no surgeon's scalpel can reach.

Crisis Textline ; *CrisisTextline.org* ; Text # 741741 (in US and Canada)

Chloe Alessandra Henkel

Did you know that when I began to shake
and only halfway-sleep
more often than not
they tested my blood?

I suppose they wanted to see if there was something there
that I didn't know about,
something lurking beneath the surface
causing all these pressing problems.

Did you know that I was actually disappointed
when they said my blood
was all right?

I wanted them to find something, a quick, easy, fix.

I know better now, I do.
I have learned to love myself as I am,
and to love all of the strings connecting to the things
that I might be,
even if many of them are coated in a fine film of fear
(slowly, ever-slowly waning, but there nonetheless).
I have learned,
but back then I didn't know if I would,
and I was so much sadder for it.

So if this is your first appointment
your first blood test
your first time wondering
what's making you hurt the way you do
I just want you to know
that no matter what it is
you will be okay
pretty soon.

If you're struggling, please reach out ; (Further resources listed on pg. 258)

Sick Days

A tip for when you go in:

Take a deep breath. Then another.
Then, try to be honest
as much as you can.

Therapy / treatment / reaching out / help
is one of the best things
I've ever done for myself.

And it's so much easier for them to help
if they know what you're up against.

You don't have to say everything at once, but
say what you can
and don't be afraid
to ask questions.

Above all just know that
they really are here to help.
They're not there to judge you
or to make you feel like shit.
They'll take count of your wounds
and find bandages to fit.

And even if this doctor, this therapist, this place
doesn't end up feeling right
for your bones:
you can switch.
Try another.

Don't stop until you've gotten the help you need
to bring you home.

Crisis Textline ; *CrisisTextline.org* ; Text # 741741 (in US and Canada)
Chloe Alessandra Henkel

Or if you're not here for an appointment at all
that's all right too.
Maybe you're just here
to visit me!
Did you bring a balloon?
Really, it's okay either way.
Why you're here doesn't matter
(unless you want to share).
I'm just glad to have a hand to hold
and an ear to pour oceans in.
Do you mind
staying a while?

I'VE FELT THESE THINGS AND SURVIVED

If you're struggling, please reach out ; (Further resources listed on pg. 258)

Sick Days

I've felt these things and survived.
More than that, I'm glad I did—glad I survived, I mean.
I survived and became happy.
I survived and became whole.
Or maybe I discovered that *whole* is something
that I've been all along.
Either way,
I've felt these things (and more)
and survived them.
So, in case you were in doubt:
you can survive
whatever it is
you're struggling through
too.
And I'll be right there on the other side
with a hug, a bottle of water,
and a bed for you to rest in
the second you do.

Crisis Textline ; *CrisisTextline.org* ; Text # 741741 (in US and Canada)
Chloe Alessandra Henkel

This is what I currently look like on paper:
GAD w/ Social Anxiety Disorder

Does it tell you anything, everything, or
nothing at all?

What does this diagnosis mean
in terms of everything
inside of me?

If you're struggling, please reach out ; (Further resources listed on pg. 258)

Sick Days

Words feel inadequate. Not all words, of course. I love words, love books, more than anything. But my words seem to fall short. As in, they fall onto the page like a wad of gum sticks to a shoe: the flavor and the color is there, but the shape and the texture is all wrong. But once they're on, I can't seem to pull them off. Do these words mean anything to you?

I have a confession to make: I want to part oceans with these words. I want to heal and adventure and write lyrics with these words. I want to love and be loved with these words. But right now I feel like I have more *want* than *words*. More lust than talent. Do these words feel true to you? Is it unfair to want to be famous when I'm not even sure I'm good at what I do? And how much of me is just the self-doubt talking?

I'm writing this in my bed, by myself, at night. In my room in my parents' house. So I guess if you're reading it, hearing it, seeing it, these words must mean something. They must have reached someone, somehow.

Right?

Crisis Textline ; *CrisisTextline.org* ; Text # 741741 (in US and Canada)

Chloe Alessandra Henkel

I call myself an artist
but my only vision right now
is 'don't burn out.'
I'm so scared to end up
twenty years older
with my dreams on a shelf.
I'm crippled by the uncertainty
that's burrowed into my bones
and made them its home.
But maybe uncertainty
isn't entirely a bad thing
because if it weren't for uncertainty
I wouldn't have written this poem.

If you're struggling, please reach out ; (Further resources listed on pg. 258)

Sick Days

I am brimming with uncertainties,
awash in the tide of my own mind
and it is all I can do to keep from
spilling
over.

But you'd never guess
how deeply buried
(drowned, *man down!*)
inside of myself I am
just by looking at me

because as much as I sputter and shake
from the lack of air in my lungs,
my body
(so accustomed to a lifetime
of more water than air)
remains perfectly poised
so as to appear to be
afloat.

I am avoiding eye contact.
I am picking away at my fingernails.
Get up, get out of bed.
I am pretending to have gone deaf.
I am wondering how hard I would have to pretend
for it to actually happen.
Maybe then, people would stop bothering me.
You're going to miss the bus.
I'm thinking I would love nothing more.
Why don't you like school?
I'm wondering what there is to like about it,
and contemplating saying so
before I remember I'm supposed to be pretending
to be deaf.
I am wondering how much difference there is
between pretending something is true
and it actually being true.
If I curl up under the covers
and pretend I am not here,
can anybody prove
otherwise?
Can I become deaf
if I learn to pretend so perfectly
that nobody contradicts me?

If you're struggling, please reach out ; (Further resources listed on pg. 258)

Sick Days

You know what I thought today? I thought that I am a terrible, terrible person. That's one of the hardest things to deal with: the thought that I am simply a terrible person.

Because for me, right now, guilt doesn't move the way it does for other people. Or what I imagine it does for most people. Though I've been told this isn't a good way of looking at it either. That there is no *me* and *them*, no *me with my weird head* and *them with their normal heads* because the truth is nobody has a perfectly "normal head" and there's not really anything wrong with that either, I know. But maybe you can overlook all of that for a moment, since I have a headache and I'm tired of trying to justify myself. Myself and my aching head.

I imagine that the guilt in other people's heads is like a conveyor belt. It moves in, it's neatly processed and packaged, and it moves out. Just like that. I want my mind to be a bit more like a happy, nicely working conveyor belt, but it's not there yet. Right now, it feels more like a garbage chute. Or a conveyor belt that's not working because it's all jammed up but it's trying to move anyway, which is only making it worse because the one or two packages that are too big to move are in the way, making it convulse in ways it's not supposed to and when I finally get them off and out of my head, they come back later. Sometimes minutes later, sometimes days, months, or years later, with the same potency, they cripple my conveyor belt.

These things could be anything. It could be that I stole a piece of candy as a five-year-old. It could be that one sad boy whose heart I broke when I was seventeen and didn't know any better but tell myself I should have (which, of course, only makes me think that every time I've had my own heart snapped was payback; *who am I to be sad?* I deserve it), that friendship I ruined, the fact that I don't get good grades, that I cried in front of a friend for too long (*such a burden*, I tell myself I am).

It can be all of these things, or something new I've never thought of, but sometimes it pops into my head and suddenly I'm breathless and I'm crying and you'd think I'd ended the world single-handedly by the kind of guilt and the kind of shame I carry in my body.

Am I a bad person? What really defines a bad person? Is a bad person what you see, when you see me? *Do* you see me?

Yet I know and I know and I know that *it is the anxiety talking. This is the anxiety talking, and not me.* Why does the anxiety talk to me, the way it talks to me? And why am I only now learning to talk back? (I have so much catching up to do).

If you're struggling, please reach out ; (Further resources listed on pg. 258)

Sick Days

One perk of being with me:

When I tell you
you've made my heart skip a bit
you'll know that I mean it literally.

You'll know that you can give me
a certain look
or a word
and make my heart
grind to a halt
for one earth-shattering second.

Because apparently heart palpitations
are romantic or something.

Crisis Textline ; *CrisisTextline.org* ; Text # 741741 (in US and Canada)

Chloe Alessandra Henkel

Friends, family, teachers, strangers:
they all keep looking at me
like they expect me to know how to talk to them
without stuttering.
Like they expect me to know how to dress myself
in something other than black hoodies and
sweatpants.
Like they expect me to know how to work,
how to smile,
how to stop shaking and apologizing and sweating
so much.
I know that they expect it
and that I should be able to do it
but I don't remember how.
It's not that I'm not trying.
It's that I'm trying my hardest,
and it hasn't changed a thing.
My heart is still trying to beat its way out of my
chest
and I am still falling short
in every way possible.
Can somebody please tell me
how to breathe?

If you're struggling, please reach out ; (Further resources listed on pg. 258)

Sick Days

I ache and ache and ache sometimes, but that's all right. I know that I've ached to the bottom of my throbbing heart in ways I thought I could never remedy a million times before. I know that if I breathe and remind myself that this is impermanent, it *will* pass. I remind myself that all of these raging emotions are symptoms of being human. And, in my case, symptoms of being human salad-tossed with symptoms of a disorder. The disorder that is not me, but is a part of me. The disorder that isn't my fault, but is mine to control. For me, for today, control sits in finding my fears on a list of symptoms, reminding myself that they're real, and that other people feel them too. They're real and they're a part of the human-salad that is me and my psyche. In this way, aching often makes me strong. I know that it stings, but I know that I will survive it. I know it burns and churns, and that every time I feel it, I can tame it a little bit more, push it out a little faster.

Crisis Textline ; *CrisisTextline.org* ; Text # 741741 (in US and Canada)
Chloe Alessandra Henkel

I sink into the sofa
across from my therapist's desk
and rattle off my to-do list of things
I don't know how I'm going to get done.

I tell her I can't imagine
dragging myself through this week.
She tells me to stop trying to
and says that instead
I have to learn to see
the forest for the trees.

Trees, which can't be taken in all at once
but can be navigated or cut down with ease
if you look at them
one *(one tree, one task, one class,*
one thought, one worry)
at a time.

Trees, which really aren't so scary
after all
in the end.

If you're struggling, please reach out ; (Further resources listed on pg. 258)

Sick Days

My thoughts taste like television static,
bitter foam in the mouth
and I wonder if I'll ever be able to focus
again.
It's not that I'm not trying to
it's just that I can't seem to find
the muscle to flex
to bring things back
into focus.
I'm fading
like an old shirt that's been through the wash
one too many times
my outline is here
but I'm a little too fuzzy around the edges.
I don't know how to bring me back
but I promise that
I really am
trying.
And I promise that I'll get it right
eventually.

Chloe Alessandra Henkel

I am running from myself.
She terrifies me sometimes.
She has invisible skin, a spine like a bluebell stem,
and she looks nothing like the person I drew
in my kindergarten art class
when the teacher told us to draw a picture
of who we thought we'd be when we grew up.

I am running from myself
and I am running from everybody else.
I am running from expectations
and everything they've come to mean.
All of my sweat and tears and late, late, nights
have already been wrung out of me.
I have nothing left to give.
But apparently, this is only the beginning
of what life is going to take from me.

I am running from my own life
and all of the responsibilities that come with it.
My legs are tired from all of this running
and I'm seeking asylum
at the nearest sad-kid refugee camp.

I am burning the candle at both ends
hoping something, anything, will catch me
before I fall.

If you're struggling, please reach out ; (Further resources listed on pg. 258)

Sick Days

Am I defined by my mistakes?
Or can I be more than the messes I make?

There might be an answer
to the questions in my throat
But I'm stranded here, nowhere
and going under without a life boat.

I've been told I'm judging myself
much too harshly
but I have no intention of stopping.

Crisis Textline ; *CrisisTextline.org* ; Text # 741741 (in US and Canada)

Chloe Alessandra Henkel

These days
all it takes
is the smallest thing
gone wrong
to shatter me.

If you're struggling, please reach out ; (Further resources listed on pg. 258)

Sick Days

(Trigger Warning: Mention of wounds/blood)

I am famished and raw-hearted
Humiliated by the things I said
before I knew you were tired of listening.

These wounds keep bleeding through bandages
and re-opening themselves
splitting skyward
like dry, cracked, desert earth
parched at the thought of you.

I am not nearly as invincible
as I like to pretend to be
when I turn out my night-light
and sleep with the closet door
open a crack.

Crisis Textline ; *CrisisTextline.org* ; Text # 741741 (in US and Canada)
Chloe Alessandra Henkel

Anxiety – something that happens when my lungs are no longer my lungs.

Depressive Episode – something that happens when my chest is nothing but an empty cavity.

Trichotillomania – something that my hands do when they're no longer my hands.

Mental Disorder – something that happens when pieces of me start disappearing / something neon-green to me that nobody else seems to be able to see.

If you're struggling, please reach out ; (Further resources listed on pg. 258)

Sick Days

(Mild Trigger Warning: Self-harm, Addiction)

I'm a flirt with candy cigarettes
touching them against my lips.

I love the aesthetic of cigarettes
but hate the smell of ash
and gag at the thought
of letting something outside of me
poison me
slowly.

I don't need another way to get addicted to pain,
no more battery acid to corrode my bones.

I give myself under-eye bags with cheap
eyeshadow
so you'll think it's all a game
but when I wipe them away
the color stays.

I started taking cynicism like medicine
and I've forgotten how to stop.

Remind me who said being sad was cool again?

Crisis Textline ; *CrisisTextline.org* ; Text # 741741 (in US and Canada)
Chloe Alessandra Henkel

(Mild Trigger Warning: Self-harm)

I am imploding in a burst of fireworks. A single speaker-cracking bass drop. A city-shattering earthquake. It's the worst kind of adrenaline rush. A roller-coaster plummet that I didn't sign up for. I can't tell if I'm sinking or flying. I'm sweating, excessively. I go for a glass of water, but my hands are shaking and it slips to the floor. Did it break, or did I? I can't see clearly. *Who pressed the self-destruct button?*

Now I am taking a breath and trying to channel this energy into *less destructive* impulses.

I'm breathing deep and I'm cutting my hair and I'm scribbling on myself with magic marker until I've lost all but an inch of skin and I'm screaming along to songs at the top of my lungs and I'm taking photos of myself in bright red lipstick and I'm running down the sidewalk and I'm eating sour candy until my tongue is raw and I'm making my best friend push me around the dollar store in a shopping cart and I'm

learning to live with the way my heart is
jack-hammering the walls of my chest
like it doesn't know what to do with me.

(I don't get any work done today.
But who could really blame me?)

If you're struggling, please reach out ; (Further resources listed on pg. 258)

Sick Days

Everyone I knew has replaced me.
I'm wasting myself away
failing to be loved.
Everything I've done is empty
if you won't even look at me.
I don't know how to express myself publicly
but I'll strip down to nothing on paper
if that tells you anything.
All I want is someone sitting here with me,
and is that really so much to ask?

Chloe Alessandra Henkel

I used to make a ritual out of self-loathing
Reciting a slew of
I-couldn't-possibly-hate-you-more-than-I-do
& *I-don't-even-want-to-look-at-you*
to the collection of sins I found in the mirror
each night.
But I've since come to think that my biggest crime
was the way I mistreated myself
at the time.
I was even younger than I am now,
still a child, incomplete,
still learning to walk on my own two feet,
so to speak
and now
I wash my face in acceptance each morning
and, on a good day,
even self-love.
I fill journal pages like they're going out of style
and hand the weight on my chest
off to my therapist each week
because I
deserve better
than letting my own anger and briars
swallow me.

If you're struggling, please reach out ; (Further resources listed on pg. 258)

Sick Days

Please hold me, I'm terrified.
Tell me I'm going to be
all right.

Maybe it's wrong of me to beg,
to open up and show my cracks
but I don't want to keep fighting myself.

This is it, this is me
asking for help.

Crisis Textline ; *CrisisTextline.org* ; Text # 741741 (in US and Canada)

Chloe Alessandra Henkel

I am so rotten-sick of raging against the world
but the only thing I know to do instead
is to go back to picking myself apart.
Is there anywhere else
for all this anger
to go?
I am so smothered by the weight of myself.

If you're struggling, please reach out ; (Further resources listed on pg. 258)

Sick Days

I'm throwing myself at the page
like drunk men throw darts at a dartboard
and little kids play mini-golf:
recklessly abandoning myself
in favor of falling into hardcover arms
and throwing myself at this rock-solid wall
over and over, again and again
hoping something sticks
and ignoring the way bruises bloom across my body like
fish coming to the surface of my skin
hungry for food.
I'm a perfect example of what is said to be
Einstein's definition of insanity.
Will you miss me if I vanish between these pages?
I don't know how much of me will be left
when I'm done
emptying it out like this.
Do you like me?
Do you know me?
Tell me about me.
Not because I'll know if you get it right or wrong
but because I'm hoping you'll throw
enough ideas out here
that something ends up sticking.

Crisis Textline ; *CrisisTextline.org* ; Text # 741741 (in US and Canada)

Chloe Alessandra Henkel

I begged the doctor to give me a pill
and cure me.
Instead she told me
I needed therapy.

Why can't I be normal? I whimpered
wishing she could just pull up a chart
and point to whatever was broken in me.

I didn't know it then
but I would, someday, eventually,
thank her.

I would someday, eventually
remember what seemed to me to be
a death sentence
as one of the things that saved me
from just that.

If you're struggling, please reach out ; (Further resources listed on pg. 258)

Sick Days

There is so much darkness inside
my snow-cold body.
I don't know how to turn the lights back on.
I think I did, at one point
but I really, truly, don't anymore.

Crisis Textline ; *CrisisTextline.org* ; Text # 741741 (in US and Canada)
Chloe Alessandra Henkel

I read like my life depends on it.
I read because
at times
it does.

But I have yet to find
just the right set of words
to describe this
blue-skied sadness
or the numbness in my hands
in those deep-winter moments when
I really start to think I might
float away.

My heart speaks in a language
lacking translation
so this is as close
as it gets.

If you're struggling, please reach out ; (Further resources listed on pg. 258)

Sick Days

I can't seem to scrub this anger out of
the whites of my knuckles.
Again and again and again
I am thrown to the floor
by people who know
my mouth is too tender,
too much a place for flowers,
to toss back anything
but the most gentle plea
to be kinder to me.

Crisis Textline ; *CrisisTextline.org* ; Text # 741741 (in US and Canada)

Chloe Alessandra Henkel

If there is a proper way to feel hunger, I'm doing it wrong. But I'm not sure that there is. Hunger is a constant emotion, a chasm in my stomach saying *'give me something, anything, more than this!'* Hunger is the way I need to write and write and write and write, even when I already have a thousand pages I don't know what to do with. I am helpless in the face of it all. Sometimes my hunger feels bigger than I am. Sometimes I wonder how to keep it from eating me whole, and I come up blank. *Hunger. Hunger. Hun—*

If you're struggling, please reach out ; (Further resources listed on pg. 258)

Sick Days

Maybe I'm tired of people trying to convince me I'm
"not that crazy"
because I *feel* "that crazy"
and if I'm not
then that's just one more thing
my mind is lying to me about.

Maybe I'd rather throw myself a pity-party
than pull myself up by my bootstraps
because pulling myself up is exhausting
whereas pity-parties involve macaroni and cheese,
blankets,
and self-pity —

Self-pity, which is the closest thing to self-love
I have at the moment.

Maybe it would be good for me to realize
it's "not that bad,"
but I don't think I'm ready for that kind of a shock just yet.

Anyway,
who wants to feel bad for me
with me?

Crisis Textline ; *CrisisTextline.org* ; Text # 741741 (in US and Canada)

Chloe Alessandra Henkel

My mind gets tied in very complicated
knots.
Do you know how that feels?

I am constantly terrified
of breaking things.
The dishwasher whirrrrrs a few pitches higher
than usual
The lights in the living room flicker out again
The dryer shivers and
shuts down with a shudder
and I worry that the repairman
will charge all of our arms and legs
only to open them up
and find my hair & teeth
clogging every pipe / tube / wire
and I worry
and I worry
and I worry again.

I am still learning that I am not
the problem that I think I am.

If you're struggling, please reach out ; (Further resources listed on pg. 258)

Sick Days

I'm slow-dancing with sadness
and loving every minute of it
with the same tender affection
one lends photos
of people who weren't always strangers.

Sadness holds my hands
then pulls away again
leaving me with band-aid fingers, hangnail stubs
and words that don't leave my lips
the way I want them to.

I am having a love affair with sadness.
He is horrible
but oddly romantic.

I hate him
but have to admit
he consistently leaves me breathless.

Crisis Textline ; *CrisisTextline.org* ; Text # 741741 (in US and Canada)

Chloe Alessandra Henkel

(Mild Trigger Warning: Suicidal Thoughts)

Depression is the dart that hits my chest
dead-center
when I chirp to my friend
that *I managed to shower today*
for the first time in five days!
and her first reaction is
Ew, that's a long time to go
without a wash.

Depression is feeling too tired to even fathom
blowing out the candles on next year's birthday cake
because you really can't find enough breath in your lungs
for today.

Depression is wing-clipped birds
unable to understand
why they can't fly
when the sky is right there.

And yet depression is not
the bed I will die in,
only the cot I find myself in
during this brief stint in the hospital.

Depression is not all
atrophy and downfall,
it's re-building my way up
to the 50-pound-dumbell
until I'm strong enough for 60, 70, 80, 90, 91, 99, 100.

Depression is a lot of things
but it's not going to be
the end of me.

If you're struggling, please reach out ; (Further resources listed on pg. 258)

Sick Days

I am a seashell split down the middle.
All you see are the cracks in my surface
wondering why I couldn't be perfect
and smooth enough to slip into your pocket
without taking a second to think about
the waves I've found myself tossed around in
and all of the treacherous places I've been.
I am damaged, but I don't regret it.
I am broken, but the cracks
are where all my stories spill out.
You can still hold me to your ear and listen.
I am still bursting with the sound of the ocean.

Crisis Textline ; *CrisisTextline.org* ; Text # 741741 (in US and Canada)
Chloe Alessandra Henkel

I crack my teeth in the middle of the night
staying up and reading alone.

I wonder what it'd be like
to have someone to share 2 a.m. with again.

What did I do to deserve all these empty hours?
And what am I to do with them
now that I have them?

If you're struggling, please reach out ; (Further resources listed on pg. 258)

Sick Days

I know I'm not supposed to blame myself
for the people who "just don't mesh with me"
or for the stack of *it's not you, it's me*'s
pressed between my diary pages.

But I can't help but think that if I were perfect
everybody would want to hold my hands
and pick up the phone when I call.
Everybody would want to be my friend
and I wouldn't have this problem.
And that if they don't
there *has* to be something less-than-perfect about me.

I buckle at the knees and fall like a downed tree
at the first sign of rejection *(imperfection)*.
It seems to be happening daily lately.

I wish I knew how to make someone want me.
And I wish I knew how not to feel like I needed to.

Epiphany:

Maybe everyone else were perfect,
they wouldn't make me
feel like this.

Maybe I'm not the only person
who's a mess.

Maybe it's time to stop trying to please everybody.

(Trigger Warning: Trichotillomania)

I don't know how to show you that this isn't pretty
without making myself feel ugly.
So I doll it up as best as I can
pinning pastel ribbons in my hair
as if that changes
the bare&weedy patches.
Only then
it looks a little too nice.
Nice enough that I wonder if you're getting the picture
or if you'll ever understand the way it stings,
the way it's ugly.
And so I muss it up and try to wear it out with pride
pride in my throat, and comfort aside
tripping at the thought of stares
the second I step outside.
I decide to wear the bows and the hat and the ponytail
after all.

If you're struggling, please reach out ; (Further resources listed on pg. 258)

Sick Days

(Trigger Warning: Thoughts about death, Suicidal thoughts)

I drafted a will at fifteen.
I mapped it all out in my diary.
I didn't have much to put in it yet.
I am still breathing.

I won't insist you cry for me,
just let me paint your mind sometime.

My body is crooked but I mean so well.
Every window I pass reeks of broken glass
and I know in my bones
I'm the reason.

I am not a seasonal rainstorm.
I am a weather pattern that is really just a solid line
because it storms and pours here, in my mind, all the time.
I am still breathing.

I am glad to be breathing.
I used to wonder how it feels to die too often.
Now I am spending
all my time breathing
and being glad to be
breathing.

I've told my parents to cancel my life insurance.
I have no more time for hypotheticals.
I plan and I plan and I plan
to survive.
I plan and I plan and I plan
to be alive.

Crisis Textline ; *CrisisTextline.org* ; Text # 741741 (in US and Canada)
Chloe Alessandra Henkel

Everything looks so small
when you're this far above it all.
I take a breath
but don't exhale.
There are a million ways to say 'I love you'
but not one of them is good enough for us
in this moment
so I'd rather let the street lights and the silence
fill the spaces
where voices turn in absence slips.

Whatever you do, please don't fall.

If you're struggling, please reach out ; (Further resources listed on pg. 258)

Sick Days

        I get a little blunt around the lips
when it's late like this.
My every other word is a hiccup
and I wish you had the sense
to stop pouncing on the aftermath.
I am not perfection and
I cannot have it
expected of me
no matter how desperate
your heart may be.

Crisis Textline ; *CrisisTextline.org* ; Text # 741741 (in US and Canada)
Chloe Alessandra Henkel

The thing about sadness is that it's
a riptide.
It's all-too-easy to go from thinking
you're just dipping your feet in
to being pulled out
further than you can swim.

Do I really want this?
Or am I just
getting out too far again?

If you're struggling, please reach out ; (Further resources listed on pg. 258)

Sick Days

Do you know what it feels like to
drown?
Because I do.
I drown every other minute on a bad day.

It starts with a tightness in the chest
a body screaming *'I'm all out of breath!'*
Then you start to feel
a little dizzy, a little numb
washed away like sea foam.
Only you're still here
in the parts of you that know
you're in a body
and not a vacation home.

Your heart says *'hold me'*
and guts you when you
can't/don't/won't
and when you really can't stand it anymore
you gasp
you sob
and just when you think you're about to choke
the ride screeches to a stop
and you remember how to float,
just like you always have.
Just like you always will.

There are two things most people don't know about it:
they don't know how much it can hurt / how deep it can go
or they don't know
that on the other end of it
you *will* find your way
to the surface again.

Crisis Textline ; *CrisisTextline.org* ; Text # 741741 (in US and Canada)
Chloe Alessandra Henkel

It's beginning again
I told you
in a voice
that was a few sounds short of a whisper
(nothing but a brief, brief flicker)
just before the world went dark
and I was sucked under
all over again.
I am so tired of vicious cycles.

If you're struggling, please reach out ; (Further resources listed on pg. 258)

Sick Days

(Trigger Warning: OCD, Health anxiety, Suicidal thoughts)

Two weeks ago today I cried in the kitchen
while my family told me that it was very unlikely
that my organs were failing.

I am eighteen and basically healthy
but after a scrape
that's left me with a scar-scratch-scar
on my finger
I had to take *(mild)* antibiotics.

So, of course I decided to read every
potential side effect on the bottle
(just in case)
and when I found myself feeling
a little off-kilter
I decided that acute organ failure
was the most probable cause.

Okay, that's not quite right.
I knew in my head it was probably
something I ate or my period, one day late
or a stomach that just cramps up sometimes
but the anxious part of me decided that the best way
to prepare for the worst
was to read enough articles on organ failure
to pass med school
and, when that didn't cut it,
to cry in the kitchen and force my poor family
to tell me that my organs weren't failing.

But the truth is,
that's not even terrible
compared to some of the thoughts I've had.

Crisis Textline ; *CrisisTextline.org* ; Text # 741741 (in US and Canada)

Chloe Alessandra Henkel

Sometimes I get these thoughts in my head and
sometimes the alarms start going off in my brain
and for some reason my it decides to protect me
from these scenarios
(ranging from somewhat probable,
to sudden acute organ failure
at age eighteen)
by making me shake and sweat and cry
and unable to concentrate on anything else
or by telling me that it would be better
(easier, more predictable)
to end things myself
(than to wait for organ failure
or the humiliation of standing up to perform a poem
only to be booed offstage
or the horror of writing my whole life
only for my work to be forgotten when I die)
to take me down, unsuspecting.

Anyway, I want you to know that if this is you
and you're obsessing over things that nobody else
seems to think about:
I'm fighting it too.
You're safe here, and I don't think you're all-that-weird.

If you think you're crazy,
then I'm crazy like you, too.

Oh, and that bad thing you're so worried about?
It's probably not happening.
Just for the record.
And if it does? We'll deal with it then.
Okay?

If you're struggling, please reach out ; (Further resources listed on pg. 258)

Sick Days

I don't know how to explain this.
Everybody looks at me like I should
(and maybe I would if I could)
but I really truly don't know how.
This is the one place where the words
let go of me.
They don't follow me here.

Here, I am more *Piccasso* than *Van Gogh*
more *Monet* than *Manet*
all shapes and colors with nothing solid in sight.
I am an abstract painting
of something in flames
a string of words in a lost language
that feel so good slipping off the tongue
that you can't tell if it's a blessing
a curse
or a completely nonsensical verse.

I'm a tongue with nothing to say
or a pen that's spewing ink
and none of this makes any sense
to any of you:
the straight-faced friends and family
who are standing outside my door
and breaking a sweat
trying to make sense of me.

Crisis Textline ; *CrisisTextline.org* ; Text # 741741 (in US and Canada)
Chloe Alessandra Henkel

Fear has a mouth the size of a lake;
it swallows me without flinching.
They ask me how it feels
and I tell them to hold their breath
until it hurts.
Then I tell them to try to imagine
that the pain doesn't go away
after exhaling.

If you're struggling, please reach out ; (Further resources listed on pg. 258)

Sick Days

I tried to throw in the towel and tell the world
to go on without me today.
I said I would be staying in bed
both because I was so very tired
and because I didn't think it would miss me today, anyway.

The first thing the world sent to contradict me
was my dog
whining like the sky was falling
because he'd finished all of his water.
I pulled myself up, poured him a fresh bowl
and collapsed back into my covers
convinced that my one and only job was done.

The second thing the world sent to contradict me
was my best friend
in desperate need of homework help.
I picked up the phone
and double-checked her answers.
Then I turned out the lights
and told her I had to go, just in time for lunch.

The third thing the world sent to contradict me
was a squirrel
scratching at the empty feeder outside my window
in a frenzy.
I gave in, got up, marched outside, fed him
and before I could sneak back into bed
my mother asked me to keep an eye on the oven for her.

I guess the world needs me today
after all?

Crisis Textline ; *CrisisTextline.org* ; Text # 741741 (in US and Canada)

Chloe Alessandra Henkel

(Mild Trigger Warning: Suicidal thoughts)

I feel helpless. This world is spinning too fast on its axis, and part of me wants to do nothing, nothing at all but fall into the grass, stare at the sky, and fade. Part of me thinks I don't have a place here at all, and I'm tired of making messes. I'm tired of the way I'm always accidentally breaking things. But I will remind myself again and again to take a breath. And another. And another. That I belong here, and I will overturn every leaf, challenge every lie that's made its way into my mind, and take a moment to look at every beautiful thing on this Earth if that's what it takes to remind me of that, because I am not giving up, damn it. Not now, not ever. I'm here and some way, some how, I'll find a reason why. One that sticks. I swear I will.

If you're struggling, please reach out ; (Further resources listed on pg. 258)

Sick Days

(Mild Trigger Warning: Self-harm)

I hate you.
No, I don't hate you.
I hate me.
I'd like to be able to hate you
but I still can't find a way to.
You're my poison of choice
every time.
I keep reminding myself
that I don't deserve the way
you curdle my skin with a touch
but for whatever reason
it still won't sink in.
There is a fine line between
selflessness and self-harm
and I walk it every time I forgive you.

Crisis Textline ; *CrisisTextline.org* ; Text # 741741 (in US and Canada)

Chloe Alessandra Henkel

Your friends and my therapist both
warned me
you would be a handful
but I told them I turn handfuls into mouthfuls
and eat them for breakfast
(like bolts and nails and Froot Loops, all in one bowl)
and besides, I adored you and
you adored me and
I didn't want/need/want to know
anything more than that.

But now you're saying it was me who
took our sidewalk cracks and made them canyons
only neither of us can seem to put a finger on
exactly what it is I'm supposed to regret
because
as far as anyone can remember
this explosion was caused by your finger
on the nuclear trigger
while I stood by
trying to piece back together
the peace treaty you took a knife to.

Your friends and my therapist both
warned me
loving you would be something like
putting my mouth on the top of a bottle of bees
but
I'm no good at hearing things
I wish weren't true
and I signed the

I-know-what-I'm-in-for waiver
as fast as I could just to shut them up, and now
each letter in the fine print

If you're struggling, please reach out ; (Further resources listed on pg. 258)

Sick Days

has given me a paper cut.
So maybe it is my fault:
not because I broke you or
shattered us
the way you'd like to say I did but
because I never should have let there be an *us*
to begin with.

Crisis Textline ; *CrisisTextline.org* ; Text # 741741 (in US and Canada)

Chloe Alessandra Henkel

Even the plants on my windowsill
have started to look at me
like they know something's wrong.
You see, plants know all the tell-tale signs:
they see the way I'm wilted,
shrunken into myself.
They notice my drooping-leaf hair
and the way my trunk has thinned.
They ask me
if perhaps what I need
is a little more sun.
I tell them you were my sun,
and now you're gone.

If you're struggling, please reach out ; (Further resources listed on pg. 258)

Sick Days

I think I'm depressed again?
It's hard to tell for certain sometimes.
It sneaks up on me
(a little closer with every message I put off
answering)
like a song that I haven't heard in a while
but suddenly find myself humming…
and *boom!* it's stuck in my head.

My vision is halfway grayscale and
everything slightly bleaker than I remember it.
I can't say for sure that I'm sinking
but the ground is soft
and there is mud creeping up
the sides of my sneakers.

At least when it hits like a freight train
I can say I'm depressed for certain.

Crisis Textline ; *CrisisTextline.org* ; Text # 741741 (in US and Canada)
Chloe Alessandra Henkel

(Trigger Warning: Trichotillomania, Body Image issues)

Hair falls like rain
into a puddle on my pillowcase
and a new bald spot is climbing the side of my head
like ivy.

For a second,
I let myself hate myself for this.
Then I push the thought away.
I deserve kindness,
now more than ever.

What will it take for me to remember
that I am more than my hair,
my skin,
and the body I'm in?

If you're struggling, please reach out ; (Further resources listed on pg. 258)

Sick Days

I want to touch every bump on your skin.

To run my fingers over
every last bit of texture

To kiss every red spot
until they're all stained darker with lipstick.

It pains me to think you truly believe
they're anything other than
blindingly lovely.

Crisis Textline ; *CrisisTextline.org* ; Text # 741741 (in US and Canada)

Chloe Alessandra Henkel

All of my fingers are broken and bruised
from blatant misuse
and clinging to things that I should have let loose.
I scrape stars from my fingernails
and let them fall like hail
onto bedsheets that know me a little too closely.
I'm staring out the window at 5 a.m.
with knots in my stomach again.
Do you know how it feels to sit perfectly still
with your head between your knees
and still feel like you're spinning?
It's not so much a *dizzy spell* as it is a *dizzy storm*.
It hits me like a meteor shower
and I have yet to find an umbrella strong enough
to hold it off.

If you're struggling, please reach out ; (Further resources listed on pg. 258)

Sick Days

I hate myself.
I hate my life.
I hate, hate, hate until my face turns blue.
I can't feel my face, my fingers, my feet, anymore.
I'm numb all over.
This isn't a poem.
I'm not a poet anymore.
Go home, go home, go home.

Crisis Textline ; *CrisisTextline.org* ; Text # 741741 (in US and Canada)

Chloe Alessandra Henkel

The panic is immobilizing.
A punch to the gut, a swift surrender.
I am vibrating
shaking ever-so-softly all over
and can't quite feel my body.
I'm behind a wall of thick, cold, glass
suspended a little bit above it all.
No, I can't *snap out of it!*
It's snapping me to pieces.

This feeling is somewhere between
rain washing the pavement clean
and a sudden power outage.
One moment, I am fine.
The next, I am lights-out
and all the neighbors are asking why
my windows went dark
and why I don't just flick on a light switch.
It feels like nobody sees how hard I'm trying.

My hands shaking so hard
that I can't write or balance food on a fork
or hold the instruction manual
that came with the generator:
'What to do when you've lost power.'
I might not be up-and-running for a while.

If you're struggling, please reach out ; (Further resources listed on pg. 258)

Sick Days

I didn't realize I was the kind of person who would rather not hear back
than receive a rejection letter
until today:
when I received
my first two rejections!
in a span of ten minutes.
Each one,
a sucker-punch to the gut
laced with niceties.
And now all I can think is
I will never be successful, I will never be okay, I have to scrap everything I've written, I have to scrap everything I haven't yet, I can't do this, I'm worthless, worth less than the paper I write on, I can't breathe, can't think, can't—
and my chest is caving in
under the breath-excavating pressure
of every opportunity that hasn't been
presented to me.
Because if I'm not good enough to write
then what am I good at?
What am I?
Who am I?
I have wanted this as long as I can remember and yet
the second I get pushback, I don't push back
I
fold.

Crisis Textline ; *CrisisTextline.org* ; Text # 741741 (in US and Canada)

Chloe Alessandra Henkel

My chest is so heavily weighted
with a tangle of fishing wire
stone sinkers
and rose petals
that I cannot straighten my spine.

My eyes are swollen lips
without a face to kiss
and my lips are chapped and dry
without a teary eye to wet them.

I sit in bed and try to piece together
where to go from here
without a map at which to look
or feet with which to walk.

If you're struggling, please reach out ; (Further resources listed on pg. 258)

Sick Days

I slipped out of classes, out of lectures, out of outings
like a shell, out to sea
for *sick days* and *doctors' visits*
for *unspecified ailments*
with shaking hands
stuffed in my pockets
to hide them from view.

And now you're here
spitting in my face
telling me that clearly
I was making myself
depressed / anxious / a stain on the carpet
for attention.

The worst part of all is that
I can't think of a single word
to explain what this really is to you.
I can't think of a way to explain it to someone
who wants so badly
not to understand.

*You will never know
how wrong you are.*

Crisis Textline ; *CrisisTextline.org* ; Text # 741741 (in US and Canada)

Chloe Alessandra Henkel

Seriously, doesn't it suck
that you can be sick as anything
but so many people
will deny it
because it's not something they can see?

The stigma around mental disarray
is eating away at me.
But I bite back
taking comfort in the fact
that every day,
people are learning.

Every time I stand up for myself
I chip away at a little piece
of the stigma surrounding me.

And every day another doctor
another survivor
another person on a mission
comes out
with an article, a song, a study
that further weakens it.

Like so many things that sting
this *stigma*
isn't permanent.

If you're struggling, please reach out ; (Further resources listed on pg. 258)

Sick Days

I'm sorry for disappearing off the face of the Earth.
It's not you, it's me.
Really and truly.
Whenever I think of you
I want to give you a hug.
If you lived a little closer
I'd invite you over
and ask you
to sit in my silence with me, but
you're so far away and
as much as I adore you
when I think of picking up my phone
or writing back to you
I feel too tired
and too dull.
It feels terrifying and
I do not have a responsible bone in my body,
so I don't do it.
Instead, I'm sending you this poem to say
I love you, and
I'm sorry.
I hope this isn't hurting you
and I hope that you don't mind
waiting for me
because I will be back
eventually.

Crisis Textline ; *CrisisTextline.org* ; Text # 741741 (in US and Canada)

Chloe Alessandra Henkel

(Mild Trigger Warning: Intrusive thoughts about death)

It's not that I'm bored,
it's that I don't feel
fulfilled.
I have a lack of fulfillment and
a lack of opportunities for fulfillment.
That, and the gravity is denser in my chest
than it is everywhere else.
My heart beats off-beat more often than it should
and I'm terrified that it's going to stop
before I get the rest of me started.
But I guess it will stop someday.
After a few years of having daily panic attacks
because of that fact
I became pretty aware of it.
Hearts stop.
But that doesn't mean I can't make the most of
(*or, on days like this, as much as I can of*)
the time I have until mine
runs out of time.

If you're struggling, please reach out ; (Further resources listed on pg. 258)

Sick Days

I feel broken. Shattered, scattered.
Too tired to keep living like this.
Every fiber of my body opposes motion.
It's hard to remember a time when I didn't feel
sick / diseased / ugly.
I'm not even sure that my friends still like me.
I'm in a constant state of crying,
feeling like I'm missing something.
Every whisper I hear feels like a dagger in the back
*(because surely everyone is whispering about me
and how much they hate me).*
I used to be the person who always laughed too loud.
Now I don't remember how to laugh at all.
Sometimes I think I want help,
other times I think it'd be better to be left alone entirely.
I'm falling, I'm falling, I'm falling.
I've been *falling* for so long
landing sounds like a fantasy.
I would love to run away.
To find a field and stay there.
To go somewhere
where nothing is expected of me.
Somewhere with lots of daisies and blue sky
where nobody asks me *why* I'm crying, *why* I'm lazy,
why I've changed so much, so suddenly.
Where people stop verbalizing all of the questions
I'm terrified and tired
of asking myself.

Crisis Textline ; *CrisisTextline.org* ; Text # 741741 (in US and Canada)
Chloe Alessandra Henkel

(Trigger Warning: Intrusive thoughts about death)

I have times where I think *Oh-No-I-am-going-to-die* constantly. I used to not want to go to school because I couldn't stop thinking *What if I die before I graduate, and this is all I ever do?* I mean, there were a lot of other reasons for the not-wanting-to-go-to-school thing, but that was one of them. I thought *even if this relationship / friendship / job / education / thing that I have lasts, I'm going to die sometime, and one of us will die first, and then it will be over.* I would walk down crowded halls and panic, wondering how people could be walking / talking / laughing knowing they all had the same terminal disease I did: a lifespan, a limit. Seconds *tick-ticking* away. I felt like screaming. I felt like warning them. I was swamped by this ever-present feeling of seconds slipping away. Every single moment was a spending of time that didn't seem worth the price.

And, like with most things, I'm not telling you this so you'll start to freak out too, or because I need you to pity me.

I'm telling you this because I want you to know that this isn't how it has to be. That I've felt that, and I've lived through it. I don't want to die any time soon. I know that I could, but it's statistically improbable. I know that I still want to make the most of this moment, to do things that make me feel okay and proud *right now*, but that it's okay—good, even—to plan for the future. To get educated and start projects, *thoughts of freak accidents cutting them short be damned!* I know that as long as I'm smart, and I'm reasonable, I'm doing the most that I can to stay alive, so other than that, it's no use wondering just when and how I'll die: it will happen eventually—hopefully and probably not for a long, long time—with or without my permission. With or without me dwelling on it. So, once I've taken the precautions I can, why in the world should I stop living now in light of the fact that yes, eventually, I probably will die?

If you're struggling, please reach out ; (Further resources listed on pg. 258)

Sick Days

I know it's not as easy as a finger-snap to fix
any of these things.
Believe me,
I've had two years of therapy so far
and I'm *so much better*
but I'm still working
on me.
And I'm definitely not here to try to cure you:
I'm a patient not a doctor, but
it's okay for us to comfort each other.
I have and do
live through struggles, too.
I'm okay with enduring
whatever you're going through
with you.

Chloe Alessandra Henkel

(Trigger Warning: Suicidal thoughts, Self-harm, Self-blame, Suicide of a friend or family member)

I'm going to tell you something that's hard to hear, but I wish someone had told me way before they did: if you're the type of person who tries to care for people, this is especially directed at you: you, with the flowers in both hands, you who still hasn't learned to put your air mask on first.
It is so kind of you to help others where you can,
but it's not your job to play therapist for a friend.
I have seen so many angels
blaming themselves
for the clouds, the suicidal thoughts, and the scars
that have worked their way into those around them.
It is so good of you to listen
and offer support where you can
but don't do it so much
you end up
with open-calloused hands.
At some point you have to know
that they are *them* and you are *you*.
That you're not to blame for what other people do.
You can hand them your love
(as long as you save yourself enough)
and you can hand them hotlines and resource books.
You can even ask for help for them
if they're in danger and you have a chance,
but I want to tell you
as someone who has, at times,
refused to let people in
and at other times
has been the person with hands full of
guilt / blame / shame
standing on the other side of the fence

If you're struggling, please reach out ; (Further resources listed on pg. 258)

Sick Days

thinking I *could have done more, should have done more,*
should be protecting them, need to save them, deserve the
anger or coldness or quiet they send my way:
There is nothing to forgive.
You care so much, you love, and you are kind-hearted,
I know that you are.
You're allowed to mess up
and there will be times where even if
you do everything right
people won't accept it
won't accept you
won't accept the help you want to give.
At some point it's up to them and only them
to choose the life they want to live.
You may help,
but you are not *responsible for* anyone
other than yourself.
When those you love
—or those you used to love,
those you've moved away from—
are struggling
it does not mean you've failed.
Sometimes things just happen that way.
Sometimes others have rainy days.
You can lend an umbrella
(as long as it won't leave you
soaked and chilled and sopping wet yourself)
but you can't take the blame for the rain.
Okay?
There is nothing to forgive.
And even if you're still convinced that there is:
I forgive you, I forgive you, I forgive you again.

Crisis Textline ; *CrisisTextline.org* ; Text # 741741 (in US and Canada)

Chloe Alessandra Henkel

I hurt so very much!
but they say
'You're okay'
as if that's enough
to make the seas of serpents
surrounding me
fade into the nothingness that they appear to be
to the unexperienced outsider,
watching me blindly,
treating me like a child
who screams that their closet and bed
are crawling with monsters.
Dismissing me as I'm falling to
p i e c e s,
sending another bright-red ribbon
a flare of pain
shooting through my chest.
And yet
no matter what they may say
I know
that my struggle is valid.
And that I will survive it
with or without the help
of people who refuse to acknowledge it.

If you're struggling, please reach out ; (Further resources listed on pg. 258)

Sick Days

(Trigger Warning: Trichotillomania,
Body image issues)

I am so fed up with being a dartboard for opinions
and unsolicited advice.

No, I don't care
how pretty you think my hair used to be.

No, I don't want to cover it up
I want you to stop staring.

Oh, really?
I never thought of "just stopping" before.
I guess I'll have to try that.
Maybe I should fire my therapist
for not coming up with a solution
that simple.

No, I don't want to take off my hat for you,
I'm comfortable with it on.

Whether I cover up or show it off,
I can't seem to get away from feeling like
everybody's staring at me.

It's like fame, without the benefits.

I should start charging for ad space
on the back of my head.

Sometimes I panic for no particular reason. Or if for a particular reason, a reason that I wouldn't always find worth panicking over, but today I do.

Today I'm wondering if I'll ever be loved. Loveable. Is there a scale on which we can weigh our worth? Can I know how close I am to the line of *"worth loving"*? I wonder if it's fair to ask someone to hold me when I'm a sniveling mess, if it's really okay to put myself on them. I wonder how I can ever be loved when I can't currently go a full day without a meltdown at the thought of it.

It's days like these I remind myself that *I am young, so very young.* I am so very young and I don't need to know how to be loved every minute of every day, I don't need to have everything together; I would, in fact, be a rarity if I did. I am so very young and even if I weren't, it'd be okay to be messy, because we're all kind of young in a way. We're younger than we could be. Younger than this flawed, lovely, galaxy.

It's okay not to have it all figured out. Someday, I'll get enough of it down. And maybe, just maybe, it's okay to be loved even when I'm not all the way put together. Because that's a little bit (or, maybe even a lot) of what love is: putting each other together. Having someone to hold you when you smile *and* when you cry. Even when the crying is a lot. I

remind myself that I'll get through this, and someday— *someday* —I will be happy and someone will be holding me and I will remember that I used to be sad and scared, and used to doubt that I'd ever stop being sad and scared. I'll remember these things, but they won't hurt me anymore. They'll make me feel brave.

If you're struggling, please reach out ; (Further resources listed on pg. 258)

Sick Days

Sometimes I am more apology than girl
and I have nothing to show for it
but the bruises on my knees
from falling down one-too-many times,
the biggest problem here being that
I never quite pieced together
how exactly a person goes about
picking themself back up.

Chloe Alessandra Henkel

(Trigger Warning: Trichotillomania)

There is hair
scattered like fallen leaves
across my pillow case.
I pull strands of it away from my lips
every time I try to sleep.

There is hair
like wet snakes
slithering around the rim of my sink,
leering at me.

There is hair strewn across the floor
like old newspapers
or streamers from a party
I wasn't invited to.

No matter how much I clean up
more always seems to appear.

If you're struggling, please reach out ; (Further resources listed on pg. 258)

Sick Days

I just want a hug.
No, I don't remember my name.
Do you need it?
It doesn't matter at this point.
I'm lonely, okay?
I'm an astronaut without oxygen.
There's nothing for me in the air around me.
I'm a beached fish or a drowned bird.
I'm imploding, constantly.
Do you get it yet?
I'm lonely and I wish you would hug me.
That's all you really need to know about me.

Crisis Textline ; *CrisisTextline.org* ; Text # 741741 (in US and Canada)

Chloe Alessandra Henkel

There are clouds reflected in my eyes
as I stare at the sky
watching planes crash outside.

I stand at the overhang
hands fluttering softly.
You ask me if I'm trying to fly away.
I tell you I would if I could.
But I stay, and you do to.

So tell me where it hurts.
I'll believe you.
I'll listen.

I'll hand you my headphones and turn up the volume
to help you drown out everything you don't know
how to keep handling.

I don't know how either of us are going to find our way
out of this
but I know that I'll hold onto you
until we do.

If you're struggling, please reach out ; (Further resources listed on pg. 258)

Sick Days

At some point we're going to have to

Stop drawing hearts
around bullet wounds.

Stop treating cliffside strolls
like slow dances.

Stop making music out of
the rattle of the china cabinet.

At some point we need to stop
romanticizing the pain
and   let   it   go.

Crisis Textline ; *CrisisTextline.org* ; Text # 741741 (in US and Canada)

Chloe Alessandra Henkel

On one hand,
I don't want to make everything about
struggling.
I don't want to hot-brand
"mental illness"
onto my face
and become
a poster child for it.

On the other hand,
A part of me,
the part of me that was told
it wasn't real, I didn't know a thing about it,
the part of me that struggled in silence for so long
wants to talk about it
and wants to make sure
she is heard.

In both hands,
I hold a future
a narrative
which I may or may not lead
eloquently.

If you're struggling, please reach out ; (Further resources listed on pg. 258)

Sick Days

I am bright green, sick with envy
at the way opportunities seem to sneak by me.
I can't seem to get my feet on the ground while
everyone around me looks like they've been found.
I cake makeup over mayhem
try to look a little less sour-lime
and a little more happy-for-them,
but rejection
failing, falling, crawling in the mud that is
not knowing where you're going
or what you're meant to be
is a bitter pill to swallow and I can't seem to help but
go green in the face with the sickness that is
seeing everyone else scrambling into first place
while I keep throwing myself at walls
only to find that I just can't stick to
or stick with
anything.
Somehow I thought I'd never be
the starving artist I look in the mirror and see.
Right now I swear I'd like to be
anyone but me.
Please, *please, please*
trade places with me?
Or at least hold me down while I scream.
Piece me together when I'm so clearly
bursting with chaos
breaking out at the edges
of every last seam.

Crisis Textline ; *CrisisTextline.org* ; Text # 741741 (in US and Canada)
Chloe Alessandra Henkel

I
am
no
longer
inspired:

this
above
all
is
terrifying.

If you're struggling, please reach out ; (Further resources listed on pg. 258)

Sick Days

Crack me open and all you'll find
are mothballs and apology notes.

What would it take for me to be good enough?
What can I do that would matter to you?

I used to have a roof
but all the shingles have been torn off
by this unexpected change of weather.

I am the human equivalent
of blue skies shut away in dust-covered totes.

I only wish someone else wanted to open me again.
I am still trying to find the hands
to re-open myself with.

How did things end up like this?

Crisis Textline ; *CrisisTextline.org* ; Text # 741741 (in US and Canada)

Chloe Alessandra Henkel

It's not that there aren't things I
could / should / would
be doing.

It's just that the sluggishness
is spreading over me
like cobra venom,
seeping into every inch of me
and making my body
heavy and numb
(ripe for eating)

and even the water
on my bedside dresser
feels so very far
out of reach
and no matter what I try
my shaky fingers
aren't moving.

If you're struggling, please reach out ; (Further resources listed on pg. 258)

Sick Days

I've heard them called *thought spirals*
or *thought trains,*
trains of thought that
the second you get on
whisk you away at full-speed.
Call them whatever you want.
All I know is that I want to get off of
whatever kind of mental ride I'm on.
I want to go home.
I am getting nauseas and dizzy.
Can you feel the ground shaking?

Crisis Textline ; *CrisisTextline.org* ; Text # 741741 (in US and Canada)

Chloe Alessandra Henkel

Nobody is listening to me.
This thought, sharp and cold, sends me spiraling.
I am upset. This is an issue. Nobody's listening.
I try to steady my breathing
but the phrases *it's not that bad* and *just deal with it*
are rattling around in my head.
I feel like a spinning, spinning, spinning top.
I try to breathe / breathe / breathe / again.
I tap my pencil against the table.
Focus. Breathe.
Somewhere, somebody is slurping a drink.
I flinch
and rub my hands across my ears.
It's too loud in here.
I focus on tapping my pencil.
On breathing.
On stopping the train of thought that has me
crashing
crashing
crash—
Stop.
I'm doing so well this week.
I can keep it up. I can move past this.
I know this is hard. I have every right to feel the way I do.
Eyes, prickling with tears.
But I also deserve to feel better. To make it through.
I can do that, too.
I breathe softer. Steadier.
I can do this.
I force a smile. Move a pencil across paper, making sparks.
All anybody else sees is me, sitting by myself
writing, stopping, sitting here, wrapped up in my own head.
But I know I just fought myself and won.

If you're struggling, please reach out ; (Further resources listed on pg. 258)

Sick Days

I feel a little too exposed
going back and seeing how often I write
from a first-person point of view
everything speckled with *me, me, me* and *I, I, I.*
Are you still here, still reading?
I won't blame you if you aren't
or if you've gotten this far and want to stop now.
You can take a break, put the book down.
I'm going to try (and fail) not to take it personally
if this isn't your kind of thing
because, to be fair,
I'm not even sure if it's my kind of thing.
All I know now is that I
can't seem to stop writing.

Crisis Textline ; *CrisisTextline.org* ; Text # 741741 (in US and Canada)

Chloe Alessandra Henkel

I am a cocktail of lighting and self-loathing.
I run screaming from myself
on-fire and flying
crashing with the recklessness of a stray bullet
into whoever makes the mistake
of crossing my path first.
Do you know how it feels
to attract casualties like a magnet?
Sometimes I wonder how many people watching me
aren't here for me at all, oh no, they're here for the show!
I draw spectators like a house fire.
People who would never admit
that they're halfway-enjoying
watching me tear myself to pieces.
Why do so many people only start watching
when you're in pain
and the pain
is loud and fascinating?
I love the spotlight
but I get tired of feeling
like a walking, talking, social experiment.
There is snow falling outside my window now,
and it is colder than the hands I use
to hold myself,
because I am a sheet of ice
crashed shattered and scattered across the road
like glass
like stars
like constellations and
on days like today
I glisten so brilliantly,
so much like candles on a beautiful, belated, birthday cake
it's hard to remind myself that I do still deserve *(& need)*
to be swept up and melted back together
after all.

If you're struggling, please reach out ; (Further resources listed on pg. 258)

Sick Days

Like all true lovers, the world and I
are frequently at odds.

Like even the most star-struck of couples
we are still learning
how to live with each other
each of us knowing all the while
that we can't exist without the other.

We are always at each other's throats
but we're both
absolutely vital to one another.

We have the epitome
of a love-hate relationship.

Crisis Textline ; *CrisisTextline.org* ; Text # 741741 (in US and Canada)

Chloe Alessandra Henkel

(Trigger Warning: Body Image Issues,
Trichotillomania/Hair-loss)

I drag my fingers across the mirror
meeting eyes with an angry stranger
with hacksaw hair and a sandpaper face.
Not-me, not-me, not-me.
I leave smudges on cold glass as I pull away.
She follows me everywhere.
She's in every reflective surface,
from store windows to rearview mirrors.
She's reflected in the way people look at me
(so different from how they did
when they thought me to be *cute* or *pretty*).
She's there, sitting on my chest
drinking the breath straight out of me with a curly straw.
She's standing behind me while I try on
tight little shirts and baggy pants
whispering *"what do you think you're trying to do?"*
She's pouring grease in my hair while I'm sleeping.
She's in my ear when we listen to love songs,
telling me I'm not *pretty enough* for love.
She is so angry with me.
She is so *mean*.

Seven years of bad luck might not be as bad
as leaving the mirror as it is: unbroken
(if that's really what it is to begin with).

If you're struggling, please reach out ; (Further resources listed on pg. 258)

Sick Days

Today I am infinitely sorry
I'm not more than I am.
I don't know how to make it up to you,
to learn to tie my shoes the right way
to stop tripping on every stone in our driveway.
I look at myself in the mirror
and see a painter
with paint all over her hands and face
and nothing but a blank canvas to show for it.
Do you know how screams feel
when they nest in your chest?
Because they sting like heartburn,
I would know.
Not that it's an excuse
for me, sobbing at your feet
and wasting my college tuition barely scraping by,
but I
am trying to explain myself
in the only way I know how right now:
with tight lips and written words.

Crisis Textline ; *CrisisTextline.org* ; Text # 741741 (in US and Canada)

Chloe Alessandra Henkel

Dear You,
People leave.
I've been here before and I'm here *(in the dumps, being dumped)*
right now,
and if you're still reading this
I'm going to assume that you are, too.
So, I'm going to tell you this:
It is so hard right now,
but we can get through this.
When whatever person you've tied
those blistered heartstrings to
flutters away on you
you can cry, you can shake.
I wish you didn't have to, but
if you're like I am
you won't be able to help yourself.
Once you've done that for a little bit,
Treat yourself to some ice cream.
Paint it out.
Journal.
Do whatever you do
when the world is falling apart around you.
Cry some more.
Don't force yourself into sleep.
Catch it when you can, but
if it's anything like I know it to be
it might not come when you call it.
Light your candles and kiss the stars
if you're going to be up anyway.
And maybe we—the two of us, I mean—
Shouldn't plan to drive tomorrow
if we can help it.
My eyes get a little too bleary when I cry
and my head gets lots too fuzzy

If you're struggling, please reach out ; (Further resources listed on pg. 258)

Sick Days

when I'm up all night,
so I figure I can afford to be a passenger
for a few days.
We can read books in the passenger seat,
and turn the radio on
even if it's the last thing in the world
our broken fingers feel like doing.
We can talk to each other,
talk to others,
write it out.
Maybe even learn to appreciate the view
from the ledge it feels like we're falling from.
Find a way to make it beautiful
even if it still burns
a little
Maybe I'm jumbled because everything
is still so fresh right now
but
if I could tell you anything
I'd say that you not only need to let yourself
fall freely
into the pain
but you need to be open-hearted enough
to let it catch you,
too.

Crisis Textline ; *CrisisTextline.org* ; Text # 741741 (in US and Canada)

Chloe Alessandra Henkel

(Mild Trigger Warning: Self-harm)

I am more than this mistake.
I am going to be okay.
I'm still dizzy, I'm a jewelry box ballerina:
spinning, spinning, spinning
I try to calm down my fingernails
as they burrow into my arms:
crescent moons on a mission.
I am imagining that I am invisible.
I am constantly reminded that I am not invisible.
I am constantly being seen, but not *seen* as in *known,*
seen as in *eyes-on-skin,*
seen as in *judged.*
How do I convince the whole world to blink at once?
How do I earn a split-second
in which
I'm free from perception?

If you're struggling, please reach out ; (Further resources listed on pg. 258)

Sick Days

I'm onstage and also
having a panic attack.
Sorry,
that's probably not why you're here
or what you expected to hear
but it's true.
My breath is very shallow and
I think I'm fading out
I'm having a panic attack, so
I understand if you want a ticket refund
and your money back, because
I'm supposed to be performing for you but
this spotlight is blinding
I'm sweating like a water bottle on a hot day,
like a rainforest,
like snow in the sun
and the truth is
I always tend to get these attacks
at the worst of times.
Not with reason, not with rhymes
I don't control them
(if I did, I'd run them out of town!).
But I don't control them, not entirely.
In fact, once I forget to breathe
they control
me.
They grab onto my knees and rattle me—
I'm giving them too much power again.
It's psychological warfare at its finest
and the wrong side of my head is winning.
My therapist tells me to
not give it so much power.
Not to let this bad voice in
when I can help it
(and she tells me how I

Chloe Alessandra Henkel

can help it)
but we all know that
regardless
it's really very hard
which is why I'm standing in front of you
shaking
and stuck in a loop of
panic! alarms! ding-dong-ding-dong-*don't
leave just yet*
really
I'm just getting started.
Wait, no,
that didn't come out quite right.
What I mean is that I'm just learning how to
breathe
in and out and in and out
again.
So I'm asking you
to please stick around
while I figure
it out?

If you're struggling, please reach out ; (Further resources listed on pg. 258)

Sick Days

Lie on the floor with me?
The ceiling is flawless today.
I won't say that the spinning stops down here
only that it's softer, more enjoyable
like riding waves instead of swimming against them.
If you close your eyes
you can pretend to be anywhere,
though I like to keep them open
and let myself go breathless
at the way the afternoon light
sneaking through the window
looks from this angle
right here.
I'm going to reach up to touch the dust bunnies
in that sunbeam now,
so get ready to do the same thing at the same time
just in time for your hand to collide with mine.
That way
we can pretend it was an accident
and we're still not sure
if the other person meant it.
My heart will race
but maybe yours will too
and you'll be so busy trying to steady it
that you won't be so rattled by the loud sound of mine.

Crisis Textline ; *CrisisTextline.org* ; Text # 741741 (in US and Canada)
Chloe Alessandra Henkel

How do you make friends?
I'm asking for a friend.

Do you think that if my friend
wanted to be your friend
you would want to be her friend?

Maybe you can sit and talk with me
while you think about it.

And maybe when we're done
I'll leave you with her phone number
just in case
you decide
you might like to
give her a call.

If you're struggling, please reach out ; (Further resources listed on pg. 258)

Sick Days

Do you know how it feels to distance yourself
until you can't remember
the sound of your best friends' laughter?
Have you ever stood outside the circle
you used to be in the middle of
fidgeting with the rim of your soda cup
and wondering what went wrong?
The funny thing about "growing apart"
is that it's so much harder to apologize and fix things
because there's not one set thing, one divide
to apologize for.
The other funny thing about it is that "growing apart"
sounds so gentle, so natural
but the burn that I feel when I think of it
makes me think it's anything but.
I've always hated parties
but I've also always thought that parties
are something I could like if I had a little luck
or tried hard enough.
Anyway, what I mean to say
is that I'm sorry I've been distant lately.
I wanted to explain it to you, to show you how I felt
but it's getting kind of depressing, so I'll end it with this:
I'm glad you still invited me
even if I don't do great with
parties and things.
It's not you, it's me
and I'm working on me.
Maybe this is awkward or too forward
or something along those lines
but I'm tired of pulling back and watching people slip away
without saying anything.
I might come off all wrong,
but at least I'll be able to say I tried this time;
I want to learn how your laugh sounds again.

Crisis Textline ; *CrisisTextline.org* ; Text # 741741 (in US and Canada)
Chloe Alessandra Henkel

I still have ups-and-downs.
But I don't hate them
like I used to.

I still have ups-and-downs
but that doesn't mean
I regret
how far I've come
where I've ended up
or where I'm going.

If you're struggling, please reach out ; (Further resources listed on pg. 258)

Sick Days

(Trigger Warning: Suicide, Suicidal thoughts, Suicide jokes)

Why I Will Never Laugh at a Another Suicide Joke:

I don't care if I "ruin the fun" anymore.
I will never not reply with "are you okay?"
and sliding you a list of hotlines
like a love note
because
most people don't joke about suicide
without it flashing across their minds.

Because far too many people are called
"funny" and "relatable"
and allowed to go home alone
with a head full of dark "jokes"
and not much else to go on.
I will never laugh at another suicide joke because
I'd rather give something a little more gravity
than it deserves
99 times
than laugh and look the other way when I shouldn't have
once.

I will never laugh at another suicide joke
because I don't give a damn about being
the life of the party
if it means risking the loss of a life at the party.

I won't shame you for making a suicide joke
(as much as I wish you wouldn't)
because I know how much easier it is
to make jaded jokes than directly ask for help
but I will never laugh at another suicide joke because

Crisis Textline ; *CrisisTextline.org* ; Text # 741741 (in US and Canada)

Chloe Alessandra Henkel

there's really nothing funny about
picturing you slipping through the sidewalk cracks
with every joke you crack
on the walk home.

So for everyone who's asked
or given me looks like "lighten up!"
this this *this* is why
it will never be
a joke
to me.

And if you are the one joking
but meaning it as more-than-a-joke
I hope you know you can talk to me:
you don't even have to
disguise it by laughing
(although I won't judge you
if that's all you can do
for the moment, this moment).

I will never laugh at another suicide joke
because I'd rather hold you
and hear you
if you need it
instead.

If you're feeling suicidal, you're not alone.
It's possible to recover, and you deserve to.
Please reach out to
CrisisTextline.org
SuicidePreventionLifeline.org
and the other mental health resources listed on pg. 258
for help.

If you're struggling, please reach out ; (Further resources listed on pg. 258)

Sick Days

My fingers freeze
held in place over the page
as I debate what to write on my
'student introduction' assignment.
I gnaw a fingernail off
trying to decide if I should
go ahead and tell the teacher
how anxious I am
or if it'd be better to wait and see
how the semester plays out.
I want to be independent.
I don't want to be in over my head.
I don't know what I'm doing.
I'm tripping over my own feet trying
to learn as I go.
I heard the bell ring
an hour ago.

It's okay to ask for help
I write on the palm of one hand
in hopes that eventually
I won't need reminding
You're not as helpless as you feel
I write on the other
in hopes that one day
I won't be faking my confidence.
I stare at them both at the same time
and hold them like a prayer
until the ink blends together
in hopes that somehow
I'll learn how to
balance.

Chloe Alessandra Henkel

(Trigger Warning: Trichotillomania,
Dermotillomania)

Did you know that some birds do a thing called
feather-plucking
where they pull out their own hair
—I mean, feathers—
or pull at their skin
when they're under stress?

Or when they're bored
or when they're anxious
or when they're lonely, at a loss.

Did you know that I want to scoop up
every threadbare bird
and tell them all I know them better
than the rest of the world ever could?

And did you know that this isn't the first time
I've felt like a caged bird
dressed up as a girl?

(pter-o-til-lo-ma-ni-a)

If you're struggling, please reach out ; (Further resources listed on pg. 258)

Sick Days

(Trigger Warning: Trichotillomania)

Scabs dot my scalp like ladybugs
but I grit my teeth and coax myself
to forgive my sweet hands.
It's not their fault
they don't know when to stop moving.
They're ambitious to a fault
and as much as I'd like to sometimes
I can hardly bring myself
to fault them at all.

I am stronger and more forgiving
than I think I am.

Crisis Textline ; *CrisisTextline.org* ; Text # 741741 (in US and Canada)
Chloe Alessandra Henkel

I swallow concern like cold medicine:
I know it's meant to help
but I still feel hesitant.
I don't know what to say
so I let the buoys you throw me
hit me in the face
while I sink.
I'm glad to know you're there
but I don't know how you can help
any more than you do,
so I'm not quite sure
what to tell you.

Can I help you?

If you're struggling, please reach out ; (Further resources listed on pg. 258)

Sick Days

It's so hard for me to tell what parts of love
are *love*
and what parts of it are disorder.
Because apparently it's normal
to be irrational in love.
But I'm irrational in everything
and am always told not to be,
so to me
love feels a lot like
illness personified.
Only there isn't a 'cure' for it
because apparently
this is how love is supposed to be?
Mine just has a little extra anxiety…
it feels like helium to the head
and no sleep, no sleep, no sleep
because I stay up all night over-analyzing every interaction.
Obsessing over him.
I think he'd taste like limerence.
I want to know for sure.
It's a full-body static shock
that I can't seem to see through.
I call people I haven't talked to in months
just to spray paint their ears with
'I THINK I'M IN LOVE WITH HIM'
but ignore all their reasonable advice
about taking it slow
or letting him know.
I mow over red flags
faster than you can say 'regret'
but if (no, *when*) it goes South
I blame bad luck.

I wonder if my therapist is tired
of talking about boys.

Crisis Textline ; *CrisisTextline.org* ; Text # 741741 (in US and Canada)

Chloe Alessandra Henkel

I want to be loved by you
but I don't even know
how to say *hello* to you
without breaking into a cold sweat.
I saw you at the grocery store today
and now I'm here
in my room
six hours later
still blushing and beating myself up
over not coming up with a single thing
to say to you.

If you're struggling, please reach out ; (Further resources listed on pg. 258)

Sick Days

The winter sky catches me
staring out my window at her,
cloud-gazing absently
as I wonder
how on Earth I'm supposed to
connect with the people
on the other side of the glass.

I am an open spark
with no kindling
to light.

Am I the only one
who craves connection
but doesn't know where to find it?

And if not,
why can't I seem to find
other people me
to be the company
I need so desperately?

Crisis Textline ; *CrisisTextline.org* ; Text # 741741 (in US and Canada)
Chloe Alessandra Henkel

(Trigger Warning: Trichotillomania)

I've left nests of hair all over my room.
Maybe I am a bird after all.

I shaved my head this morning.
I think it's time I learned to fly.

I'm pretty sure it was the right thing for me.
I've never been so exposed.
I've never felt so
free.

If you're struggling, please reach out ; (Further resources listed on pg. 258)

Sick Days

I wonder if this is permanent. I like to think it's not. That's why I struggle to define it. Not wanting to wash it away, minimize it, when it's so loud right now. But not wanting to brand it into myself, iron it onto my metaphorical skin when I'm in the process of washing it out, unsure if it will stain or not.

In my Spanish class today, we were asked to write a paper defining ourselves two different ways. Using the word *estoy* when describing a temporary part of ourselves, and *soy* to talk about something more permanent. So which is it for me? *I am anxious, I am anxious, I am anxious.* How should I talk about my feelings? *Estoy ansioso* (I am [currently] anxious) or *Soy ansioso* (I am anxious [as a person])?

I don't know. And perhaps that's not such a terrible thing. Why is it that I always need to label things? Right now, I am anxious. I have an anxiety disorder. But I may not always. Or maybe I will. It's like a freckle, in a way. Sometimes, freckles fade. I used to have one on my arm, that I don't any more. But there's one on the back of my hand that I've had as long as I can remember.

Today I am anxious, but tomorrow I may not be. The weather changes, the colors of the sky change, and as they do, I begin to realize that perhaps I need to spend more time *accepting* and less time *defining*. I am currently staring at a tree with vivid green leaves. Tomorrow, they may turn gold or red or orange, or stay just as green. Perhaps it is an evergreen tree. The tree doesn't need to be permanently branded, afraid to change. But the tree doesn't need to be dyed or painted, pushed to change either. The tree is green. Tomorrow, the tree may be green, the tree may not be green.

(e)s(t)oy ansioso.

Crisis Textline ; *CrisisTextline.org* ; Text # 741741 (in US and Canada)

Chloe Alessandra Henkel

I don't entirely blame you:
I know you're overwhelmed and understaffed
with so many friends
like chores, like duties, like plants to water
to pay attention to
so I can't entirely blame you
for the way you ignored me
for the way I needed you and you left me
hollow and aching.
It stings like the prick of a needle
not being your best friend
when I need you,
not being your best friend when you
told me I was.
But again, I know
I'm a little needy
the black sheep of your flock
the breakdown you weren't quite ready for,
I know you didn't come prepared for
the baggage I brought and
with everyone else on board with you
there's no room for me in the luggage rack, so
maybe it'd be best for us both
if I change airlines / train tracks / travel plans
to someone, somewhere
a little more
prepared.

If you're struggling, please reach out ; (Further resources listed on pg. 258)

Sick Days

It is possible to feel as low as this
and find a way out of it.

It is as possible to feel as low as this
then go on to be glad you didn't give in.

I've seen it happen
and I've done it before.

I've done it before
and I'll do it again.

Crisis Textline ; *CrisisTextline.org* ; Text # 741741 (in US and Canada)

Chloe Alessandra Henkel

(Trigger Warning: Trichotillomania, Dermotillomania, BFRBs)

It's hard to find a particularly pleasant way to tell you
that yes, sometimes I pull the hair
right out of my head.
That I almost like the way it pops out
from the stem like
uprooting a weed
and that I look at the root and think
'that used to be in me.'
There's only so much dancing and digging
around the subject
I can do
before saying
'I am the reason for the bare area where
a garden of hair used to be'
and
'Yes, it bothers me,
but it bothers me almost as much
when other people talk about it
like it's something that should bother me.'
And as much as I hate the idea of
romanticizing things that bite
in the dark corners of my attic-head-attic
I wish there were a few more stories
about lovers pulling lovers' hands away from
faces or scalps or
wherever they're pulling from
and kissing them calm.
I feel like there should be a little more out there
reminding us that
trichotillomania and dermotillomania and other BFRBs
aren't dirty words.
They may not be the prettiest of things, but

If you're struggling, please reach out ; (Further resources listed on pg. 258)

Sick Days

I'd never say the same about the people they accompany.
No, they—we—are gardeners, are worker bees
with minds that jump and fingers that dance
(though not always where we'd like them to).
We are brilliant.
We
are
stunning.
More importantly than that
we are
trying
our
best.
We deserve representation.
We deserve
love.
We deserve
care.
We deserve the world and then some,
quite frankly.
And I hope that's what
every
last
one of us
gets.

Crisis Textline ; *CrisisTextline.org* ; Text # 741741 (in US and Canada)
Chloe Alessandra Henkel

Does this change who you see
when you look at me?
I whisper
holding my breath
bracing for impact
and reminding myself that I am worth
so much more
than whatever words come next.

If you're struggling, please reach out ; (Further resources listed on pg. 258)

Sick Days

Please be
as gentle as you can.
You'll never know about
the welts your words can leave
on skin as thin as mine is.

Please keep being
as kind as you are.
You'll never know how many times
I've worn your words to bed
and let them heal me
either.

Crisis Textline ; *CrisisTextline.org* ; Text # 741741 (in US and Canada)
Chloe Alessandra Henkel

It's not your fault
you're full of flames.
But don't let the fire
consume you.
You deserve much more
than burning.
Your future holds much more
than ash.

If you're struggling, please reach out ; (Further resources listed on pg. 258)

Sick Days

My bed is afloat in a sea of stars,
and by that I mean: I'm stuck here
because the second I step out of it
I fall into an uncertain abyss
not unlike the night sky
so I stay put
in my life-boat
and watch
as days and nights
hurry past without even stopping
to look in my window.
I lean slightly over the side
contemplating the forever
and nets of mental fishing wire
between my feet and the floor
and my bed and the door
before creeping back over to the edge
closest to the window
dipping my fingers
into the star-studded ink beyond
and wondering if someday
maybe
I too can be a part of it all.

Crisis Textline ; *CrisisTextline.org* ; Text # 741741 (in US and Canada)
Chloe Alessandra Henkel

We've become nothing but a hurt-in-progress:
a painting-in-the-making of jagged thunderclouds
and rainy funerals.
But this doesn't stop my feet
from angling towards
the strangled flurry of motions and emotions
that we are
because
I can't seem to take my eyes off this disaster as it unfolds.
I have to watch our hands
reach out and tear each other
down from the sky.
I have a feeling I'll be holding my breath
until the moment we hit the ground
if for no other reason than that
I know if I blink
I'll miss the moment of impact,
and I'm just dying to see
how far this blush-red explosion goes.

If you're struggling, please reach out ; (Further resources listed on pg. 258)

Sick Days

(Mild Trigger Warning: Mentions of death,
Mortality)

How do I become immortal?
To write something that never dies.
Would it suffice to beg you to pass this on
and tell your children to pass it on
and hope that it goes on and on?
Or wait—
Do I have to amaze you first?
Write until I hit the nail
on the head?
Write to impress
like my life depends on it?
I am envious of Shakespeare and celebrities.
I want to be seen, seen, seen
even when I no longer have hands
to feel it with.
I want to be more than just
the body that is me.

Crisis Textline ; *CrisisTextline.org* ; Text # 741741 (in US and Canada)
Chloe Alessandra Henkel

Note to Someone I Loved a Little Too Hard (Pt. 1)

Holding back feels like madness to me.
I don't believe in partial-love:
I believe in stovetops and hot irons.
I believe in the kind of burnt-cookie heartthrob
that you can't turn away from
or wash out of your mouth
once you've tasted it.
The only reason I bite my tongue
is because I don't yet know
if you believe in it too.
I am hiding within myself
for fear *(stoplight-red, devastating, fear)*
of losing you.
I am swallowing all of these flames
until you tell me
you're ready
to kiss them out of me.

If you're struggling, please reach out ; (Further resources listed on pg. 258)

Sick Days

(Trigger Warning: Blood, Needles)

A Note to Someone I Loved a Little Too Hard (Pt. 2)

I'd give you a blood transfusion
just to be a part of you
because after this collision that we are
I think you'll be needing it.
So hold out your arm and I'll take
a needle and thread to our veins.
Hold still, I swear
there won't be any pain.
We're both ambulatory, just barely
but I'd sell my soul for the legs that you walk on
just so you could be a part of me.

Crisis Textline ; *CrisisTextline.org* ; Text # 741741 (in US and Canada)
Chloe Alessandra Henkel

I give far too much of myself to everybody else
and still haven't managed to find someone
who fits me like I fit them,
someone who would do the same for me.

I could waste time blaming or beating myself up about it
but the truth is, I'm glad I'm the way I am.
I'm glad that even if I can't imagine
what it's like to be smothered in a love like the love I give just yet
I have been able to be that for so many people,
who probably needed it more than I did
if the way they hurt me
is any show of the ways they've been hurt.

Even if it didn't end well, I know
that I was a positive impact
on a lot of the people I've touched.
And maybe if I'd found my person too soon
I wouldn't have been able to provide comfort
for other people who really needed
the pieces of me that they left with.

Even when it stings
I grit my teeth as hard as I can
and try not to regret it.

If you're struggling, please reach out ; (Further resources listed on pg. 258)

Sick Days

I am supposed to be doing
school work right now.
Does anyone else wonder why this kind of education
is so draining?
I can read for hours, you see
it's not learning that's the problem for me
it's not taking in information that's my sore-spot:
it's school
and its certain classes, subjects, stuff.
It's things that I don't see the point in.

The problem with this problem is that
knowing it hasn't solved it yet because
I still need (and maybe even want?) an education,
but I can't seem to sit still for it long enough
to bring myself into focus
without feeling irritable
like I'm an ice-cream cone crawling with ants
melting in the sun
I want to get up and run
to stare out the window
to write to you again
to do anything, really, other than what I should be doing.

Anyway, what are you doing reading this right now?
Are you reading to get out of work, too?
I always used to read in class.
To read and draw and drift off, and
it's not good of me to encourage that because
there was probably knowledge I could have gained,
but lost.
There were near-misses with failed classes
which almost left me diploma-less and
swallowed in a tsunami of
why / how / fix this now

Crisis Textline ; *CrisisTextline.org* ; Text # 741741 (in US and Canada)
Chloe Alessandra Henkel

from teachers & my family, but at the same time
I'm aiming for a job in writing, art, and feeling.
Even my career
—which is what everyone
constantly seems concerned about:

it's never *'How are you?'*
it's always
'How are you going to be financially in ten years?'
If you're looking from a place away from that,
that place can be here: How are you?
Can I help you?
Do you feel okay today?
Not that money doesn't come into play,
but it certainly shouldn't be the only thing
on your mind and in your life.
It's no more important than your mind
and I hope you don't mind my saying so.

Anyway—
Even my career is in the things
I've preferred to studying
from the beginning.
But I still have to study unrelated things or
related things in formats and settings
that don't work for me
to get to where I want and need to be.
And how unfair is that?

But I'm going to go and try
to get a little more done,
and if you're someone who needs to, too:
it's okay if/when you struggle.
It's okay to think it's hard and unfair, and
I'm wishing you the best of luck in spite of it all.

If you're struggling, please reach out ; (Further resources listed on pg. 258)

Sick Days

I am putting in a ridiculous amount of work
for classes & work I feel no connection with.
Not that I have much of a connection
with anything other than headaches these days
but if I was going to
connect with something
it certainly wouldn't be
this.

Crisis Textline ; *CrisisTextline.org* ; Text # 741741 (in US and Canada)

Chloe Alessandra Henkel

Can we please normalize
having no fucking idea where you're going?
I'm sure I'll figure it out eventually
but in the meantime:
I'm sick and tired
of people asking.

If you're struggling, please reach out ; (Further resources listed on pg. 258)

Sick Days

(Trigger Warning: Aversion to touch)

Don't touch me / Don't touch me / Don't touch me / *Please* don't touch me / It hurts / Back up / I need space / Space to breathe / Don't touch me / Don't touch me / Don't touch me / Don't take it personally / I really can't breathe / Don't touch me / No, I don't need a hug or a squeeze or a hand on me / Not right now / I need a few feet of space / Don't touch me / Don't touch me / I'm sorry / Don't touch me / I wish I could build an electrical fence to get myself a little space / I wish just stating my boundaries was enough / If I don't have this body to myself, then what do I have? / So maybe I am a control freak. / If I say you're right, will you back up? Please? / And who do you think should control this body and the space around it, if not me? / Don't touch me / Don't touch me / I don't owe you an apology / I don't owe you anything / But I'd give you anything / To back up with your hands up / It's not you or me / It's everything, all at once, too much to handle, like hot sand or scalding soup to the tongue / Don't touch me / Don't touch me / *Please.*

Crisis Textline ; *CrisisTextline.org* ; Text # 741741 (in US and Canada)

Chloe Alessandra Henkel

(Trigger Warning: Self-harm)

I have scratches and bruises on my arms
from a rough night
but I, in the morning light
take them in softly.
I feel nothing but love for myself
and my body
for the heartaches it's carried me through.
I choose to assess the damage gently,
to bandage and ice myself
lovingly
and I learn
with the help of hot tea
books
and therapy
to move forward
slow-but-steadily.

If you're struggling, please reach out ; (Further resources listed on pg. 258)

Sick Days

(Trigger Warning: Climate crisis, Intrusive thoughts about death, The world ending)

Our climate is crashing and burning.
Our climate is crashing and burning.
Our climate is crashing and *burning*.
We have approximately ten years
before it's too late to undo all of this damage
being done to our environment, our planet, our ozone layer.
This is my intrusive thought for today,
but it's also a true thought
and this makes it even harder to cope with.
Because these mental-optical illusions are one thing
but what do I do
with real fires and fright?
What do I do when the real world is at my doorstep
and it truly is terrifying,
not only because of the reasons my head has made up
when it wants to find fear in shadows
but because of real-life facts like
I might die early because of climate change and
we are in a climate crisis and
the world is literally falling apart?
I have my head on the edge of my book shelf
and I am breathing heavy, trying to steady myself
fingering the spines of every book I find
but nothing calms me because
there is no manual for what to do
when the world is really and truly ending in slow-motion
and you also have an anxiety disorder.
*I need to do more, I am not doing enough,
if I don't save, fix, hold up this world, who will?*
For a second, I am no longer breathing.
For a second, I have drowned.
I am nothing but a star, exploded:

Chloe Alessandra Henkel

dust, ash, and brilliant catastrophe.
The best (and, tonight, only)
thing that calms me is to write it out.
To make a makeshift guide for you to find
when you're like me,
spiraling as you watch the clock count down
in despair as you watch everything fade:
running out of time.
Our climate is crashing and burning.
Every day, every moment, people die:
for this reason, and many others.
I could die any second
and not even know it
until it's done.
I could feel like this forever.
I could run and run and run
and never find a place to rest my feet,
never find a place to fit
never find a way to quell the aching pain
of realizing all of these things at once.
But the truth is that
I am still here and, therefore, there is still time.
Time is with us, as is life, at least for now.
At least for this moment.
And that, my love, means everything
because it means that we still have a fighting chance.
I may not be able to save the world.
But I refuse to die alive because of it.
I will live as best as I can, while I can.
Both because I believe that I—and every individual—
have the power to help, at least a little
and because if I am going to die
early, late, or somewhere in-between
I refuse to do it without being able to say
I lived as much as I could in the meantime.

If you're struggling, please reach out ; (Further resources listed on pg. 258)

Sick Days

Just because I'm not made for the triathlon that is
of media / marketing / rinse / repeat
doesn't mean I can't write up a storm.
I just wish I knew how to be heard
in this apocalyptically modern world.

Crisis Textline ; *CrisisTextline.org* ; Text # 741741 (in US and Canada)
Chloe Alessandra Henkel

I'm sorry for being so scattered.
I know I'm all-over-the-place today.
There's just so much to say
and not nearly enough space
to say it with.
I'm not used to speaking up like this.
I'm not used to knowing how to be heard.
I have so many built-up words.
And now they're
s p i l l i n g
out.

If you're struggling, please reach out ; (Further resources listed on pg. 258)

Sick Days

(Mild Trigger Warning: Self-harm, Trichotillomania)

I don't want to be defined by this. To be reduced to nothing but scraggly hair and scar-studded skin. But it seems, right now, that my only choices are to hide it, or to be known for nothing more. And I am tired of hiding. In fact, I am angry at the fact that I was ever made to think I had to hide myself. So I am showing it. I am showing everything. And if people define me by it, if they don't bother to look deeper than the headline and end up thinking there's nothing more to be than this: so be it. That's a risk I'm going to have to take. Because maybe if I show all of my less-than-perfect parts, all of this mess that I am, the next time someone chooses to show it just like I do, it won't seem as unusual. Maybe I can help make a world where people don't have to choose between hiding or being boxed in by what they're brave enough to show. Maybe spilling my guts like I do will help make a future where showing the hurt under your skin isn't so unusual that it becomes your definition.

Crisis Textline ; *CrisisTextline.org* ; Text # 741741 (in US and Canada)

Chloe Alessandra Henkel

(Trigger Warning: Trichotillomania)

I am an anxious mess
with all the aches and pains to show it.
I haven't been sleeping much lately
so I'm running on desperation
and pulling out all my hair—ouch. *ouch.*—
I'm not writing right now because I
have something to announce
(other than, perhaps, that I should be asleep right now
or that I've given myself a bald spot that is
physically half the size of my palm
but mentally as wide as an ocean
and I don't know how long
I can keep it hidden).
I'm not writing because of that.
I'm writing because writing diffuses the
time-bomb tick-ticking in my chest.
It makes the pressure a little less,
every word putting off its detonation
by another minute.
I'm writing because everything in the universe feels wrong
except for this
and this feels so right
I can't help but feel certain
that I was made for it.

If you're struggling, please reach out ; (Further resources listed on pg. 258)

Sick Days

The scariest part is that
once I start barreling down this path
being sucked into the undertow
pulling me into my chest
I really don't know how long it'll last:
it could be days
weeks
or months
before I'm washed back up
onto shore.
But I take a breath
let the current take me
and remind myself that I will be
okay, returned, brought back home
eventually.
I always have been and
I always will be.
I hold my breath
and trust the stars
in my compass heart
to guide me.
I put my trust in the tides of my life
entirely.

Crisis Textline ; *CrisisTextline.org* ; Text # 741741 (in US and Canada)
Chloe Alessandra Henkel

(Trigger Warning: Self-loathing, Feeling worthless)

For the longest time
I couldn't have passed a lie detector test
telling you I mattered.

Luckily for me—or unluckily, maybe—
99% of the population are not good lie detectors
and the 1% that are tend to turn that off
when you're telling them exactly what they want to hear.

I don't know how to describe the way it feels to believe
more than anything
that you have a net worth of zero.
And, to be honest, I hope you never need to know.
But just in case you do:
it's a bit like walking around
with a broken-mirror heart
tucked away inside an aching chest.

I talk about my chest a lot with
stress and depression
and I think that's because that's where all
the strings do—or don't—attach.
That's the place that hurts
when my pieces don't fit
like I'd like them to.

Then again, things are different now
and I don't think I could pass a lie detector test
telling you I *don't* matter, or that I'm worthless
(like I thought I'd always be)
anymore.
Not most days, anyway.
And that feels like a pretty good start to me.

If you're struggling, please reach out ; (Further resources listed on pg. 258)

Sick Days

A Note to the People I Love:

It's not your fault. It never was.
I don't know if I'll ever be able to explain
the teeth my feelings bite me with.
But the fact is that
for whatever reason:
they're sick.
And that means I can't always express myself.
It means it's hard for me to tell you what I mean.
It means it's hard for me to figure out myself.
It's not your fault I have a disorder.
Sometimes it flares up
and sometimes
it's because of something you said or did
and sometimes we need to make adjustments,
but other times
it's because of something I say or do
or because of nothing at all,
and that's okay too.
My point is that
it's not your fault I'm sick,
even when you accidentally trigger it
or happen to be around to see it.
I know nobody's perfect, and that you're trying your best.
I'm glad you're here.
We're learning to deal with things together.
I'm not holding that against you.
You're not expected to cure me.
Please don't blame yourselves
for something none of us asked for.

Crisis Textline ; *CrisisTextline.org* ; Text # 741741 (in US and Canada)
Chloe Alessandra Henkel

(Trigger Warning: OCD, Health anxiety, Intrusive thoughts about death)

I am terrified of dying.
Do you know how often I check over every creaky
joint in my body?
You can't prove that these stomach cramps
won't be the death of me.
I am deluged with a horror of possibilities.
My breath catches on my tongue
just thinking about the way
my heart is not a permanent fixture.
My ship could sink at any moment
and I'm still learning how to sail it.
I don't know what I'm doing
and I'm so scared of dying
before I find
something.
I am constantly wincing at myself
jolted awake by the realization of all of the time
I'm wasting.
Do you promise to keep on loving me
when I'm no longer blinking?
I promise to keep on loving you.
Until then,
let's both promise
to try to think only of
living / blinking / drinking air as crisp as cider.
Let's promise to only think of life.
Of living.
Of sky.

If you're struggling, please reach out ; (Further resources listed on pg. 258)

Sick Days

I am more than my shelf of home remedies
prescriptions
and doctor's notes.
I am more than all of my *I-can't* 's.
I am more than all of my sick days.

I think I forget that sometimes.

Crisis Textline ; *CrisisTextline.org* ; Text # 741741 (in US and Canada)

Chloe Alessandra Henkel

Dear Me, In the Past, Who's Feeling Hopeless

I hope you know future-you
has learned to adore the brisk air on walks.
I've found a new favorite song
(and I'm not going to play it for you until you get here).

Did you know
you've yet to even meet your future favorite pair of jeans?
And you've yet to see the best sunset you've ever seen,
or really find your passion.

You've yet to receive countless messages
from other people just like you
saying they admire you
and saying that you've helped them, too.

You've yet to rediscover strawberry ice cream
or change your favorite color to pastel blue
(blue like robin's eggs / like summer skies / like *hope*).

You've yet to meet your new best friends
or to binge-watch *Gilmore Girls* with your mom
and walk your dog with your dad
(because yes—*you* have a dog now).
You've yet to meet this boy who I can't even begin to
describe, but you'll fall right into place with once you find.

You've yet to give a performance that was so fun,
so exhilarating,
that all you could think while you were up onstage is
I'm meant to be here, I'm glad I made it, and
Remember this feeling.

So give it time.

If you're struggling, please reach out ; (Further resources listed on pg. 258)

Sick Days

Give it a day. A week. A year.
As long as it takes, really.
But start with that.
It seems like a long stretch, but it's nothing but a blip
compared to your whole life ahead of you.
Things change with time.

So give it a year.
And then some, as needed.
And while you're at it: talk to someone.
Talk to as many people as you need to
to get the help you need.

I know it seems scary and embarrassing,
but people really do want to help you.

And, more importantly, you'll be robbing yourself
if you give up on the possibility of change
instead of reaching out for help.
Because, at worst, the first few things you try
(the first therapist, the first heart-to-heart with a friend,
the first time telling your family "this isn't working")
won't change a thing.
And at best,
it'll be a game-changer.
At best, it'll help you fall in love with life again.

And since I'm from the future,
I'm going to give a few spoilers:
it helps.

Treatment helps. Talking helps. Trying helps.
Things are going to get better.
And I know you're at least as terrified
of taking that risk

Crisis Textline ; *CrisisTextline.org* ; Text # 741741 (in US and Canada)

Chloe Alessandra Henkel

than of letting things stay the same,
but it's more worth-it than you can imagine.

I promise you, you don't want to miss this
and you're more capable of getting here
than you can imagine,
so don't give up on yourself just yet.

Sincerely, You, From the Future.

If you're struggling, please reach out ; (Further resources listed on pg. 258)

Sick Days

You are not alone

as in

*it is possible to feel the things you've felt
and learn, later, to be happy again.*

It's been done before
and you *can* do it too.

I can't wait to read your success story.

Crisis Textline ; *CrisisTextline.org* ; Text # 741741 (in US and Canada)

Chloe Alessandra Henkel

Can I let you in on a secret? I guess I already have let you in on quite a few, but can I let you in on this one, too? I am in love with love, I am in love with other people, I am in love with a wonderful, romantic life of orange-sherbet skies... all in theory, anyway. I mean, I hope to have all this someday, but I still find it hard to go out. Hard to talk to people, to really connect with them, to think that they really truly like me. Which is part of the reason I love writing you. Because you're my imaginary friend, in the sense that I imagine you reading this, imagine you listening to me, and I feel less alone. I imagine you reading this, and listening, and understanding me perfectly. So it's okay if, at the end of the day, you're still like me: still a little more pretending than anything. Still in the process of figuring out how to brave the world. It's okay if you want to pretend I'm there with you while you do. In fact, I'm probably somewhere *(anywhere)* right now, pretending to be there with you, too. And maybe, if we imagine it hard enough, and give ourselves the time for the baby-steps we need to take, we'll find our way to everything we're craving, for real someday.

If you're struggling, please reach out ; (Further resources listed on pg. 258)

Sick Days

"You're too talented to be sad all the time" my mother said, as if I could Van-Gogh the sadness out of my blood—except, that didn't work out too well for him, either, now that I think about it. But there is still some truth to what she said. There were pools of talent like bottles of paint all lined up inside my head&hands&chest but it was too hard to make any use of them when I was doing nothing but staying in bed, crying into my pillow. Until, of course, I learned that even that can be turned into something. Until I learned to paint with my watercolor tears, to turn feelings into faucets into art. Until I learned to hold the hands of my feelings and turn them into something tangible, something that pulled me up into a sitting position for a few minutes because I just had to put it down on paper. A single piece of paper that turned into two and three and four thousand scribbled notes. Until I used whatever it was that my mother saw under my baggy eyes that made her think 'talent!' to bring me back to myself. Maybe it wasn't talent at all. Maybe it was life. Maybe I'm just too alive to be sad all the time. All I know is that today, a year later, I am talented, and I am not sad all the time anymore.

YOUR NEXT BIRTHDAY

Crisis Textline ; *CrisisTextline.org* ; Text # 741741 (in US and Canada)

Chloe Alessandra Henkel

Please stay alive &
care for yourself.
You don't even know it but
the whole time you've been reading this
I've been
falling in love
with you.
Falling in love with the way your hands
linger on the pages
& with the way your eyes flicker through words,
piecing them together and suddenly
understanding
& with the way you look
when a certain lyric catches your heart
& with the simple fact that you gave me a chance
to share my heart with you
and hold these pieces of you
in return.
Please know that you are
desperately
beautifully
loved.
I would not be nearly as whole as I am
if it were not for you.

If you're struggling, please reach out ; (Further resources listed on pg. 258)

Sick Days

You'd never believe you made it to eighteen
But here you are
living and breathing
now knowing you can do
the impossible.

Because birthdays aren't just about being born.
They're about all the ways
you've survived this long.
Which is something you've earned
again and again.

So when they dim the lights
bring the cake and presents
think and think and think
'I deserve this'
until you believe it.

Crisis Textline ; *CrisisTextline.org* ; Text # 741741 (in US and Canada)
Chloe Alessandra Henkel

I wish I could give you every tender song I've ever heard
even the ones whose names I don't remember.
I wish I could see the calm wash over your face
as the music floods your ears
and the rest of the world fades away.
I wish I could press flowers into your moondust palms
and scribble on them 'you are loved, you are loved.'
I wish I could squeeze your brave & bruising hands
until every last bit of uncertainty
subsides.
And I promise you with everything in me
that somebody will be lucky enough
to do this and more for you eventually.
In fact, I envy and adore them already,
for all the ways they'll get to comfort you.
Just try to hold on until then, okay?

If you're struggling, please reach out ; (Further resources listed on pg. 258)

Sick Days

I'm just going to say it:
sometimes it does seem like everybody
is anxious&depressed these days.
Which is a good thing in the way that
if you, like me, have felt this way
you're absolutely not alone in it.
But this sentiment used to make me feel
worse, not better.
Both because my mind was telling me that I was alone,
so it just made for one more thing that I felt
that didn't match up with the truth
and because it made me feel like
even the one thing that was different about me,
my excuse for the way I felt, my secret little disease
wasn't all that different after all.
But, in the words of poet Neil Hilborn,
"This is not to say you're not special.
This is to say *thank God* you aren't special."
And maybe it's wrong to quote another poet in a poem
but this is my poem and I'm doing the best I can,
and besides
these are the first words I ever heard
that made me feel like I wasn't the only one who ever had
this weird little thought of
'I would rather be alone. I would rather be special
because if I'm going to be sick
at least let me feel special
and different
because of it.'
I became a pain-Olympian
comparing myself to everyone else, trying to figure out
if I fit my anxious&depressed diagnosis
better or worse than they did.
Wondering which one of us deserved help
more.

Chloe Alessandra Henkel

Wondering who was real and who
wasn't.
I wanted to be allowed to feel like I was the only one
who'd ever felt the things I felt
because it was the only thing I knew how to do,
to feel too much, to burn like the sun
and if too many other people did it too,
then where did that leave me?
Then I wasn't special, I was just unhappy.
But the truth is this:
you are special in so many ways.
And in the way that you aren't 'special,'
in the way that you are less alone than you might think,
it's okay not to be.
It's better, even, once you get used to it.
It doesn't invalidate you
any more than one kid with a lost tooth
or one broken leg
is invalidated by another.
One of the worst things
society, instinct, or something in-between
has done to us,
the over-thinkers, the over-feelers,
and the mentally disordered, unstable, uncertain, disabled
is convinced us
that we are in competition with each other.
One of the best things we can do for ourselves
is to overturn this false belief.
We are all valid.
Our struggles, our lessons, our open-handed souls
are no less valid
whether they are one of millions
or one-in-a-million.
You and I are spun from the same messy, messy thread
and I don't resent either of us for it anymore.

If you're struggling, please reach out ; (Further resources listed on pg. 258)

Sick Days

Hey, hey. It's me. I forgive you (me) for all of the mistakes you've made, and all the ones you probably will. I know that you've messed things up. Barreled over speed bumps you should've seen coming. Hurt and tossed people who loved you a lot. Hurt and tossed yourself when you really, really shouldn't have. I know you've gained love, lost love. I know you've taken shots and you've messed them up and that there are some people who will never like you (they might even hate you) and that you are not perfect. I know that you have scars (physical and not-so-physical) and that sometimes your jokes or your words come off all wrong. I know that there are people who you might always wish would read your poems and never will. I know that you might always push a little too hard, or abandon ship just a little too soon. But you know what? I forgive you. On behalf of everyone who ever has and everyone who never will. I forgive you, not because you're a saint, but because you're a sinner of the most beautiful kind. I forgive you because you've made mistakes, and like the best of us, have grown new limbs from every one you've chopped off. I forgive you because I love you, and because you're too new to life to let all of these things that will one day seem small— or if not small, *healed* —sit on your chest. I forgive you and I love you and as much as it hurts, I'm going to try my best to give you permission to learn *(grow, garden, grow).*

Crisis Textline ; *CrisisTextline.org* ; Text # 741741 (in US and Canada)

Chloe Alessandra Henkel

I'm sad today.
Are you sad today too?
I hope you're not
but if you are
maybe I can hold
your empty hands
and we can be sad
together.

If you're struggling, please reach out ; (Further resources listed on pg. 258)

Sick Days

In case nobody told you this year:
Happy birthday!
I love you.
I'm so proud of you for all you've done
all the mountains you've crossed
and seas across which you've swum.
You deserve the world
and you'll have it, too.
I am here
to celebrate
you.

Crisis Textline ; *CrisisTextline.org* ; Text # 741741 (in US and Canada)

Chloe Alessandra Henkel

Even if it's not
your birthday
today
you're a year further ahead
than you were
a year ago today.
You deserve to be proud.
To be happy out loud.
I am here to celebrate you
and everything you've done
and everything you'll go on to do.

If you're struggling, please reach out ; (Further resources listed on pg. 258)

Sick Days

I used to think I didn't deserve
the breath that stung my lungs.
Now I look for people like me
in the corners of book stores and bakeries
thinking I'd like to spend my life with them
if I could figure out where to find them.

How did I go so long
without realizing
I am breathtaking?

I will no longer accept love
that feels terminal.

I will no longer hide my eyes
while walking home.

Crisis Textline ; *CrisisTextline.org* ; Text # 741741 (in US and Canada)
Chloe Alessandra Henkel

I don't know who needs to hear this right now,
but you don't have to keep a secret
if that secret is that someone isn't safe.
It's okay.
You can tell a supportive counsellor, friend,
family member.
It's better to have them angry and unscathed
than ruined by the secrets
they begged you to keep.
Sometimes breaking promises
really is
the best thing to do.

If you're struggling, please reach out ; (Further resources listed on pg. 258)

Sick Days

Even though I am hurting, I am so, so, happy right now. I am happy because I know that I will get through this. I know that I really do have this whole, big, life ahead of me, and that even though it's probably going to take a little time, I'm going to learn to get swept up in it and take off these weighted boots once again. I know that I am so loved, even as I keep finding myself thinking otherwise, and that there's so much out there just waiting for me. *I'm happy, I'm so happy!* I find myself thinking now, with tears streaming down my face. I'm so happy because I am determined to conquer this, I am determined to conquer all of these messy, crazy, challenges that have been placed in front of me or stemmed up from inside of me and be the best person I can possibly be. I am so happy because I know that I have time, and that I'm *going* to make good use of it. I'm so happy because I can feel, under all of the aches and wounds, that I have a future that is brighter than anything I've yet to hold, and I'm willing to work towards it, one day at a time.

Crisis Textline ; *CrisisTextline.org* ; Text # 741741 (in US and Canada)
Chloe Alessandra Henkel

My best friend asks me how I found a therapist
and said she thinks she might like to make an appointment
just like me.

I finally tell the boy I like about my panic attacks.
He still says the only thing he doesn't get about me
is the fact that I like pineapple on pizza.

My hair starts to grow back in little sprouts, sticking out.
My mom walks up behind me and tells me
it makes me look like a *punk rocker.*
I smile at her in the mirror.

My dad buys me fidget toys
and other things to calm my anxiety
and listens with interest while I explain
how each one works
and what it's for.

The teachers from my old school
send emails saying they miss me
and invite me to visit
whenever I feel up to it.

What I mean to say is that
people tend to take things
better than you think they will.

What I mean to say is that
it doesn't always hurt
to let them in.

If you're struggling, please reach out ; (Further resources listed on pg. 258)

Sick Days

I'm afraid the stardust has settled
so perfectly into your skin
that even you have forgotten
how to notice it.

If only you could see yourself from here
you'd understand
how visibly
you're shimmering.

You deserve all the love and patience and help
that you need
to let you see
the *you* that I see.

Crisis Textline ; *CrisisTextline.org* ; Text # 741741 (in US and Canada)
Chloe Alessandra Henkel

Because this seems to me to be
an all-too-common misconception
in mental health treatment
I wanted to make sure you know:

Nobody is trying to strip you
of that beautiful madness of yours.
They just want to ice the bruised parts
and make it all
livable.

You will still be art.
You will still be
colorful.
You will just be happier
and more *okay* while you're at it.

Does that sound like a fair enough goal?

If you're struggling, please reach out ; (Further resources listed on pg. 258)

Sick Days

Then again, in case I haven't stressed this enough:
life can be beautiful, life can be gravel-tough.
You don't need to be
mentally ill, sick, or in need of help
to relate to this.

You're welcome here even if you're
just somebody who's felt some of my feelings
or just another person who's fascinated by words.
You're welcome here if you're going through a rain spell
or a tsunami.
You're welcome here if you're scared for yourself
but haven't been diagnosed with anything.
You're welcome here if you're just trying desperately
to understand a loved one
who's stuck under the ice
(from the perspective of someone
who has been that loved one
I want to say thank you! for this.
The world needs more people like you).
You're welcome here if you're a doctor's-note
disordered person
or if you're
sitting in a psychiatric hospital bed as you read this.

You're welcome here if you're sick or well.
You're welcome here if you do or don't
want or need
any extra help.

No matter who you are or why you came:
sit down, stay.
The room is brighter, lighter, less hungry
with you here.
Welcome to the family.

Crisis Textline ; *CrisisTextline.org* ; Text # 741741 (in US and Canada)
Chloe Alessandra Henkel

You are not by yourself anymore.
We're here!
We're sorry it took so long, but we found you!
You're one of us now.
No more feeling isolated
by the gentle cracking of your bones.
No more wondering why
you've never had a piece of sky to call home.
You're ours and we're yours
and here,
tears can flow like rivers
and laughter is loud enough to startle the birds.
We love you more than hot tea and candy hearts.
We love you in the way that the sky
loves each and every star.
You are not by yourself anymore,
and you never will be again.

If you're struggling, please reach out ; (Further resources listed on pg. 258)

Sick Days

Pick up the phone, even if you have to stutter
I think you'll be glad you did.

Let people know what you need.
It doesn't make you a burden
(only human)
and if they really love you &
deserve the space they get to share with you
they'd much rather hear
than be left guessing.

"I need a little space."

"Can we step outside for a minute?"

"I'm a little anxious right now,
so if I seem distracted,
that's probably why."

"Could I have a hug?"

These are all
okay
(wonderful)
things to say.

You are not taking too much space.
You should be asking people
to make sure there's enough room
for you, too.

Crisis Textline ; *CrisisTextline.org* ; Text # 741741 (in US and Canada)
Chloe Alessandra Henkel

When my brother and I were younger
and we cried at every scrape and bruise
as kids tend to do,
our dad would always tell us to count to thirty
to make the pain go away,
and if I didn't work the first time
he'd tell us to do it again.

What a sweet-but-simple way to say
that sometimes all you need
is to survive the next thirty seconds again and
again
(even if all you're doing is counting each one)
to pull forward
and wait for the pain to wane.

If you're struggling, please reach out ; (Further resources listed on pg. 258)

Sick Days

I just wanted to tell you
that I think my dog would love you.
He leans against my leg
and wags his tail
every time I write to you.
And I wanted to remind you
that he and I
are rooting for you, too.

Crisis Textline ; *CrisisTextline.org* ; Text # 741741 (in US and Canada)
Chloe Alessandra Henkel

I am (over)romantic
but that's one thing
I don't want to change about myself.

I throw love like splatter paint:
getting a little bit everywhere
and making something
beautiful, irrevocable,
leaving the scene with messy hands.

I get hurt hard
when I blunder
into someone who doesn't know
what to do with a person
who is more water than stone,
but I still love the way my heart
can make anything its own.

I bite the pain
to keep the beauty
and I am doing my best
not to let tragedy taint me.

If you're struggling, please reach out ; (Further resources listed on pg. 258)

Sick Days

Come outside!
There are so many fireflies out tonight.
I'm down here, on my back, in the damp grass
and I promise you there's room enough for two.
Do you see them? The lightning bug lanterns
bobbing through the air?
They're iridescent, dancing in a way
I can only dream of understanding.
Little fairy lights, lanterns
changing the night sky for the better:
go ahead, catch one.
It's glowing in your hands
but I can't tear my eyes away from your face.
Your face all lit up with the glow of the moon
and that hushed yellow-green firefly light.
Your smile is my silver lining.
You let your little firefly go
but your hands are just as radiant
as they were when you were holding it.
Your eyes are spilling secrets
but they're the marvelous kind.
Look at all the fireflies
landing on your shoulders!
I would be a little bit jealous
but the truth is
I can't possibly blame them
for wanting a piece of you, too
after seeing the way
you light up
in the dark.

Crisis Textline ; *CrisisTextline.org* ; Text # 741741 (in US and Canada)
Chloe Alessandra Henkel

I am suffocating
at the thought of you feeling poorly.
Is this feeling really contagious
or am I just a mirror-image
of the closest heart?
I am fighting fear
with every fiber of my being
at the simple thought of you
feeling like me, on a bad day.
So when you say nobody cares
it shakes me.
I'm so glad you're speaking your mind
but I wish I could reach in
and pull the lies out of it for you
because that couldn't be further
from the truth.
I care about you
and I am you.
I will breathe easy
when you do.

If you're struggling, please reach out ; (Further resources listed on pg. 258)

Sick Days

Where do you go when you *need* not to be found?
Do you have a place where you are unabridged
in secret?
I am perfectly myself
sitting on the floor in the nearest used-bookstore
with crumpled bills in my pocket
and hardback books in my hands.
I am most myself in a quiet nook
between shelves of books of pages older than I am.
I am most myself reading to myself with lips shut
and ears open,
or reading things I've written
with lips open, opening ears for miles.
I am most myself reading the backs of cereal boxes
or the time stamps
at the bottom of my post-office receipts.
I am most myself
lost between words.
I am most myself
when I am nothing but language.

Crisis Textline ; *CrisisTextline.org* ; Text # 741741 (in US and Canada)

Chloe Alessandra Henkel

(Mild Trigger Warning: Trichotillomania)

I keep catching myself staring at people like you—people with tattered hair, or people with art-project outfits, people who stand out as *somehow different* – in public.

Then, I snap myself out of it. I try really hard not to stare, to look away, because I know how uncomfortable it can feel to always have people *looking* when you're just trying to *exist* in your own body.

But it's so hard not to glance at you again, because the second I see you beautiful, different, people, a flashbulb goes off in my head, and my mind sings *'There's someone like me!'* And I stare at you and think how cool you look, and how comfortable I already feel around you because you're different than the norm, and I'm different than the norm, and in that way, we're the same. I think about how good you look, and wish I could pull *different* off as well as you do. I wonder what it'd be like to be friends with you. I hope that someday we'll meet somewhere where I have an excuse to talk to you, and that, maybe then, I'll find out.

Anyway, I just wanted to let you know that not everyone who looks at you is thinking terrible things.

Some of them are quietly calling you *friend.*

If you're struggling, please reach out ; (Further resources listed on pg. 258)

Sick Days

*My favorite things about being
an anxious&sensitive&messymessy person:*

I can empathize with others
with the warmth of a fireplace
and the clarity of glass.

I have learned
all of the tips and tricks to handle stress
and had hours, days, years of practice
to perfect them.

I feel the things I feel so very deeply.
Once I learned not to be embarrassed by it
this too became
a luminous thing.

It pushed me off the written path:
I don't feel like I can see things and do things
the way that other people do,
so I'm inventing my own way of living
instead.
And what an opportunity that is!

I am making art out of it.
Out of the ups and downs.
Out of the formerly shapeless thoughts and
feelings.
Out of everything I see.

It's who I am—or part of it, anyway.
And how could I not love
such a big part
of someone I love?

Crisis Textline ; *CrisisTextline.org* ; Text # 741741 (in US and Canada)
Chloe Alessandra Henkel

a note to the writers, the artists, the makers:

Before you say you don't like your writing, your art, your style, or some other thing you created, ask yourself this: *why don't you like it?*

If there's a reason (it's too colorful, too plain, too short, too long, too much—or not enough—something), then that's good! See if you can change it! That's how we learn, how we make progress.

If the reason is something more along the lines of *I made it, so it must be awful. I made it, therefore, I don't like it:* then stop right there. Question this. Because this isn't a rational line of thought. And if that's the only flaw you can find in it, then it's probably actually quite amazing.

If the reason is *I hate everything I've ever made today, none of it is okay. The whole world is caving in this morning:* take a break. It's okay. I've had days like this, days where the best thing to do is take a step back. Days where your heart is tired and doesn't know how else to tell you then to hurt.

Either way, don't give up. Don't stop what you're doing.
No matter what, there is a way of overcoming the doubt that's been raised. And either way, I for one, love it, because it's something (anything) you and those beautiful hands of yours made.

If you're struggling, please reach out ; (Further resources listed on pg. 258)

Sick Days

Let's take this one step at a time.
Flutter-feet, breathe easy
let yourself take it slow.
Check off check-boxes
and cover your eyes each time they wander
down the list and linger
on all that's ahead of you because
you'll get there when you get there and
you're not there yet,
you're here!
Right here.
And all you're doing by wasting yourself away
thinking about everything upcoming,
every future road sign
is ensuring that you never get there,
or that if you do,
you do it exceptionally slowly because
you're frozen with fear and
it doesn't
have to
be this way.
Take it back.
Take a breath.
Take one
step
at a time.

Crisis Textline ; *CrisisTextline.org* ; Text # 741741 (in US and Canada)

Chloe Alessandra Henkel

Things I would tell my past-self if I could:

The first thing I'd do if I had the chance was
take her by the hands and make her practice saying
"I'm anxious, I'm sad right now.
Can you help?"
until she could look me in the eyes and say it
without flinching.
I would teach her to reach out for help the same way she
reached for the highest apples on the tree each summer:
eager with hope and with fear as an afterthought.
I would tell her what kind of people to avoid and
how to spot
who and who not to date.
Or maybe I'd just give her a list
with names of people to avoid
in bold:
it'd be much quicker that way.
I wonder, would that stop her?
Would it steer her away from all those
bad-ideas wrapped in silver linings
that she was dangerously good at finding?
I would show her how to turn her thoughts into words,
give her the gift the world gave me
so much sooner.
I would hold her close and tell her not to be ashamed
of the way her voice cracks
or of the space she takes up
and is constantly trying to shrink her way out of.
I would show her how to draw boundaries
like rivers
all around her.
I would tell her that she is going to look so beautiful
without that long, golden, hair
she let define her for so long.

If you're struggling, please reach out ; (Further resources listed on pg. 258)

Sick Days

I would hand her a pile of books to read,
books that feel like home to me.
And more than all of that, I'd tell her it gets better.
I'd tell her about
the amazing friends she'll have one day.
I'd introduce her to the boy
whose hands are going to feel like home to her,
and whose voice becomes
her new favorite sound.
I'd let her run her fingers over the pages of this book
and tell her that she's going to write them.
I'd tell her stories that she can't believe,
in which she's the protagonist.
I'd tell her a little about the hurt:
not enough to scare her worse,
but just enough to let her know
that it happens and it heals.
And finally,
I would hold her hands,
brush her hair,
and tell her that I already forgive her
for all the mistakes
I know she's still going to make
in spite of my advice.

Crisis Textline ; *CrisisTextline.org* ; Text # 741741 (in US and Canada)

Chloe Alessandra Henkel

I did it! My life might not be perfect, but *oh my*—it's amazing. I'm sitting in the car—*in my best friends' car, because I have friends now, after spending years trying to figure out how to connect and where I fit in and why it was so hard to find people to fit in with*—and we're driving down the highway and it feels a whole lot like we're flying. We're blasting the music and nobody's shooting me strange looks for putting on songs I like; we're all singing along, feeling safe enough to sing off-key and loudly. We're passing sodas and snacks back and forth and my only thought is that I'm going to try one of everything. That, and that I am so done being afraid. My chest feels lighter; softer, somehow. The breeze from the half-down windows is blowing back my jet black wig-hair and I'm feeling a little bit like a character in some old teen movie, ready to take on the world with everyone watching.

(This is just one of a million pieces of proof
that there really is more to life
than sadness)

If you're struggling, please reach out ; (Further resources listed on pg. 258)

Sick Days

(Trigger Warning: Mention of death, Dying)

If there are alternate universes
there is probably one in which
I am dead right now.
I feel so bad
for everyone who lives there.
Here in our universe
the sun is rising,
the grass is green, sopped in light,
and I am still standing, seeing it all.
Things are so much better this way.

Crisis Textline ; *CrisisTextline.org* ; Text # 741741 (in US and Canada)
Chloe Alessandra Henkel

I'm alive!
I can see the sky
whenever I want to!
I think I forget that sometimes.
I think it gets lost
in the rush of things.
But I'm alive, I'm alive, I'm alive.

If you're struggling, please reach out ; (Further resources listed on pg. 258)

Sick Days

Dear little firefly,

This world is so beautiful
with the two of us
in it.

Did you ever notice
the way the sun rises and falls
over your home every night?

And the way that
so many stars have aligned
to bring us here, together,
on Earth at the same time?

I couldn't possibly be happier
or more grateful
to have you here
right now.

Crisis Textline ; *CrisisTextline.org* ; Text # 741741 (in US and Canada)
Chloe Alessandra Henkel

This world is in love with you,
she just doesn't know how to show it yet.
Be patient with her, please?
I'm confident she'll figure it out
sooner than you'd expect.

If you're struggling, please reach out ; (Further resources listed on pg. 258)

Sick Days

It's okay to feel like you're breaking right now.
Your heart is an open-mouthed bird:
it only knows wanting.
Nothing of patience, nothing of timing,
and everything of the ache of hunger.
And who are you to blame yourself
for cracking
under the pressure
of an avalanche of absence and hunger pains?
You don't have to live
a charade of complacency:
it's okay to scream and
rip holes in the warm night sky.
Just swear you'll let it be
more revolution
than implosion.

Crisis Textline ; *CrisisTextline.org* ; Text # 741741 (in US and Canada)

Chloe Alessandra Henkel

Hidden Hearts:

I will not spend this life
hiding from the fact that I'm human.
So many of us are so used to mincing
our thoughts and our words and our feelings
into tiny, tiny, pieces
and scattering them like bread-crumb bits
throughout our own narratives
as if we have no place here.

We snatch our words out of the air
and stuff them back down our throats
because we are not to be beacons for attention.
We are tropical storms, we house hurricanes,
but we keep these things hidden beneath our skin,
silent but hopeful
because otherwise, we would be too cumbersome.

Society, friends, family, disposition:
there are so many things that we could
draw on our life maps and pin with blame
but the end result is still the same:
we are in hiding.
And we should be sick of it.

Today, I thought to myself that
I have mastered the art of apathy.
After all, I've self-treated wounds by stapling the words
I don't care right over them
and using laughter as concealer for the ones that still hurt.
I have been hit in the knees by rejection
and felt too embarrassed to talk about it.
I have been hopelessly lost
and too shy to ask for directions.

If you're struggling, please reach out ; (Further resources listed on pg. 258)

Sick Days

I have been excited!
And afraid to become an annoyance because of it.
And finally, I have become tired of it.

Which is why I have decided to step away
from my starting-position
of just-below-the-line-of-sight
one tentative step at a time.

I will make paintings
by throwing my bleeding heart at paper
and fly them from every flag pole!
I will ask every person I meet how they are
and if they have a favorite star.
I will cry in public places,
I will read horoscopes aloud on the bus.
I will turn my face up to meet the rain.
I will tell everyone I meet about my heartbreaks
and the bruise on my shin
and about how much I love catching fireflies
then watching them fly back out into the night.
This watery heart will be open.
It will be proud and held to the sky.

And I like to think
that yours will be too
and that after all we have seen
and felt
and been through,
we will not spend our lives hiding from the fact
that we are gorgeously, achingly, human.

Crisis Textline ; *CrisisTextline.org* ; Text # 741741 (in US and Canada)
Chloe Alessandra Henkel

When you're feeling worthless:
please remember
I feel worthless sometimes, too.
I don't know what to do with myself and I
can't find my value.

But I know
that those snapping-snarling-thoughts
aren't true.
They don't define me
and they don't define you.

So, if you have those same
bad-mean-thoughts
but when I tell you I have them
you still think I have value,
it only makes sense
that you still do
too.

If I matter
(and I do, I do, I do)
then you do
(and you do, you do, you do)
too.

If you're struggling, please reach out ; (Further resources listed on pg. 258)

Sick Days

There may be times when all you can do
is let the sadness, the fear, the aching
wash over you
like when you're in the ocean
and you dive under a raging wave
to avoid getting hit
and then you're
underwater
looking up
hearing the dull roar
of water colliding with water above you
so you wait
a foot or two beneath it all
until the waters are calm enough
to break through.
Until you have a chance
to meet the open sky again.
Don't be afraid to wait out the waves.
They will subside with time.
You will find a way
to come back up for breath
again.

Crisis Textline ; *CrisisTextline.org* ; Text # 741741 (in US and Canada)
Chloe Alessandra Henkel

This is me taking the time and space to remind you:

You are worth it. You are loved. You are necessary.
You are more than your mistakes.
You are more than your sick days.
You deserve to take breaks.
You have a brilliant voice. You deserve to be heard.
Your struggles and concerns are valid,
even if they seem small to somebody else.
You have an amazing future ahead of you.
You were made for more than struggling.
You are capable. You are gloriously unique.
The universe loves you,
even when she's not good at showing it.
You are a work of art. Your thoughts matter.
You can change. You can grow.
You will find peace with your regrets.
You will find peace with your past.
You are deserving of a vibrant, peaceful, future.
I'm thinking of you.
I hope you find the words that bring you home.
Your bad feelings aren't permanent,
no matter how hard they try to convince you otherwise.
Just the fact that you are here, breathing, surviving it all
is amazing and should be celebrated.
You matter.
I don't want anything bad to happen to you.
Your safety and your happiness matter.
I care about you.
You can do this. You are braver than you know.
I believe in you, and that delightful heart of yours.

If you're struggling, please reach out ; (Further resources listed on pg. 258)

Sick Days

What if you make it?
What if you really stop selling yourself short
& you stand up and read that thing you wrote
& everybody loves it?
What if you decide that
you're not going down without a fight
& you fight
& you win?
What if you decide
to change the world around you
for the better
& you work
& you struggle
but you don't ever, ever give in
& it changes
just for you?
What if you
even just for a day
let yourself think of all the ways
things could possibly go
perfectly
and they do?

Crisis Textline ; *CrisisTextline.org* ; Text # 741741 (in US and Canada)
Chloe Alessandra Henkel

Don't like the world we're living in?
Let's change it.
We are the world.
The future, the universe, the plot
is in our hands.
Here we are.
What should we fix first?

Hope grows on trees
and we're destined to pick it.

If you're struggling, please reach out ; (Further resources listed on pg. 258)

Sick Days

And when there's nothing left but scribbled fire in your head, when you're oh-so-scared of the beautiful burden that is your heart: write it out. Really. I didn't think it would help at first, but my therapist told me to try it for two weeks at a time: to try writing down the terrifying thoughts somewhere where nobody would find them. Try writing whatever went through my head, because I needed a place to put it and because I was even worse at talking out loud back then. Try writing it down and seeing if, after two weeks, I could really still say it didn't do a thing for me. I rolled my eyes because
surely

throwing a few words at my mental hurricanes would be like spitting on a forest fire, but I tried it anyway and once I started writing I
couldn't
seem to
stop.

I've filled up volumes with chicken-scratch, with *please-save-me* and *I'm-proud-of me*'s. It doesn't have to be anything earth-shattering, but wherever you are on your road, wherever you find yourself, give it a try. Once a day for two weeks. Try writing, drawing, scribbling it out. Maybe it won't do a thing for you. Maybe you'll have to try something else until you figure out what helps. But it left me with a little less burn and a little more sugar on my tongue, and so, if for no other reason than that I love you and it might help you too, I wanted to pass the recipe along.

Crisis Textline ; *CrisisTextline.org* ; Text # 741741 (in US and Canada)

Chloe Alessandra Henkel

Here, love.
Take a pinch (or a fistful) of music for your ears.
Take some books to coax you out of your head
and blankets, pillows, and plush bears for your bed.
Take hot showers and sweet, healthy, snacks.
Take a walk outdoors
and the love of a pet.
Take a paintbrush, a keyboard, a ukulele, a pen,
anything to let everything in you
out
gently.
Take a drive and time to stargaze,
take (and make use of) the phone number of a friend.
Take pictures to remember
all the moments you felt like smiling
and take the beach, take a belly-laugh, take
a warm bowl of spaghetti.
Brush your hair,
brush your teeth,
let yourself have little things.
More than anything,
make a list of everything
that helps you
both so you have it when you're sinking and
so you know how
to keep yourself up on the bright days.
Take all these little things,
as often as you need.

If you're struggling, please reach out ; (Further resources listed on pg. 258)

Sick Days

Even if you think you'll never be able to say
whatever horrible thought is running through your head
out loud,
you can think it
or jot it down
or whisper it
to this page
right now.
I give you permission,
I'll sit here and listen,
and when it's done
I'll tell you
all is forgiven.
I know I'm not right there and
I may not know you, not yet, not now,
but this book, this chunk of my chest
is right here in your hands
and you've been so kind as to listen to me,
that I'd like to do the same for you if I can,
even if it's just pretend.
Send me a thought, a mental note,
unburden yourself,
I won't judge.
Let yourself think
whatever you need to think
and know that if I were there right now
I'd absolutely hug you and say
  'this will be okay.'

Crisis Textline ; *CrisisTextline.org* ; Text # 741741 (in US and Canada)
Chloe Alessandra Henkel

I once found an injured butterfly
and taught it how to fly again.

Have you ever felt
the fine dust of a butterfly's wings?

Do you know the feeling
of soft powder dusted across your palms,
glistening faintly?

Miracles happen
in places you'd usually never think to look.

Butterflies are so small, so paper-thin
and yet they fly hundreds of thousands of miles
though sun and storms and wind.

I see the colors of a million butterfly wings
taking flight
in your beautiful, fragile, eyes.

If you're struggling, please reach out ; (Further resources listed on pg. 258)

Sick Days

You're a polaroid picture of a comet
a blazing star, frozen in motion.
I could write for years
and never pinpoint this emotion.
Your body is museum-worthy
and artists wouldn't dare try
to capture a mind so divine:
fear of failure would swallow them first.
You laugh like a seabird cries:
with wind chimes
and echoes of waves on your tongue.
I'm up in flames at the thought of you
being watered down.
So how is it, I wonder,
that you can still look in the mirror
hands up, eyes wide
and tell me
it's empty?

Chloe Alessandra Henkel

I am brimming with
alive.

I am a space heater
or a piece of the sun:
I am warmer than the air I'm breathing.

How much do you love me?
It doesn't matter anymore!

I love me. I love me. I love me.
I am shattering myself
with the force of this love.
All of my seams are leaking gold.

My dog puts his head on my feet
like he feels it. like he sees it.
like he is warmed by this love.

And I let him.
I let him love me.
He will not leave.

I finally feel like I deserve
the way he stays.

If you're struggling, please reach out ; (Further resources listed on pg. 258)

Sick Days

One thing I wish I knew about recovering
from mental disorders and emotional stings
is that it's not all-that-abnormal to feel
as weird as I did
once I started to.

Because what was life
if not the war that it was
for so long?

What was I supposed to do with all the empty space
in my head and my day
when the alarm bells and seven-hour meltdowns
died down?

Where was I supposed to go now that I wasn't
hiding under the covers?

My days had been scribbled out,
mostly composed of hiding in trenches from myself
and I didn't know what a 'normal' day
or headspace
was supposed to be.

It almost makes me itch
to self-destruct again
just to feel
a little more normal.

Long story short: even good change
can be uncomfortable.

But there are other ways to fill in spaces.
There is a way to re-discover
how to fill a mind and

Crisis Textline ; *CrisisTextline.org* ; Text # 741741 (in US and Canada)

Chloe Alessandra Henkel

run a day.
You'll find room for hobbies and
smiles
and meandering.

You might find meaning in walks through the woods
or a new pet, new friend, new sport,
new favorite constellation.

You will probably find pieces of you
in your own rubble
that you never
even
knew.

Anyway,
if you hit a bumpy patch like this,
a pitfall / a false alarm / a blank space
trying to find yourself again,
try not to let it suck you in.

Growing pains are a sign
that you're healing
and that you're making progress
again.

If you're struggling, please reach out ; (Further resources listed on pg. 258)

Sick Days

I hope things get easier for you soon.
And I hope you choose to do
whatever you can
to make them easier for yourself, as well.
Because you
of all people
do not deserve to be trapped
under the pile of dirty dishes
that suffering is.

Let the starlight
                seep in
                              to your skin.

Let it swallow up the night sky
                        and show you
                                    tomorrow.

Crisis Textline ; *CrisisTextline.org* ; Text # 741741 (in US and Canada)
Chloe Alessandra Henkel

Good morning, sunshine!
You bring snacks, and I'll drive:
we're going to an art museum,
one of the most wonderful, confusing, places on Earth.
A place that's glorious and hushed
and pieced together jaggedly.
Everything here is beautiful in someone's opinion
and ugly in somebody else's.
Everybody here either has
paint-splattered clothes and ink-coated hands
or is laughably pretentious
with faux-fur coats
and upturned noses.
Can you hear the pictures on the walls talking?
We're able to slip
unnoticed
in-between the eccentric cast of characters
trying to find meaning in color on canvas.
I think my favorite thing about being here
is that nobody questions you,
no matter how much you may stick out
as soon as you step back outside.
That, and the paintings of course:
I could look at the art all day
(if I weren't so busy staring at you staring at them).
I think this town could use more places like this.
More places anyone and everyone
can find pieces of themselves in.

If you're struggling, please reach out ; (Further resources listed on pg. 258)

Sick Days

When was the last time you took a moment to appreciate
how far you've come?
Can you take a minute and try it
right now?
You've made it through so much
and you're still here, still standing.
That alone is a cosmic miracle.
That alone you deserve to be noticed for.
That alone is cause for celebration.

Crisis Textline ; *CrisisTextline.org* ; Text # 741741 (in US and Canada)
Chloe Alessandra Henkel

I just want you to know that most of my friends are people
with messy feelings
just like me
and that I love being able to squeal with them
when things go right
and to link pinky-fingers and lead them through
the times when the hurricanes in their heads
are spiraling
just as much as I love all of the ways
that they're here for me.
And I just want you to know that
no matter how big or bold or messy
your thoughts and feelings are,
you are not too heavy for love
and there are lots of other people like us
made of open arms and searchlights
looking for someone like you to hold.

If you're struggling, please reach out ; (Further resources listed on pg. 258)

Sick Days

(Trigger Warning: Body-image issues, Trichotillomania)

This is a self-portrait in which I have no eyes to see with:

In it, I am not
the unvarnished curves of my nose
or the absent hair
my hands tore out
when they were homesick.

No, in it I am
the lilt of my voice
which I have been told sounds like sunshine.
I am the gentle caress I gladly give
to anyone who needs it
and I am hugs as big as the sea.

In it, I am kindness and the things I do.
I am a soul, and a good one at that.

This is a self-portrait in which I have just realized
that my eyes have so much to learn
about how to behave
in this eye-candy store of a world.

Crisis Textline ; *CrisisTextline.org* ; Text # 741741 (in US and Canada)
Chloe Alessandra Henkel

Other people's harsh words
don't reflect
or detract from
your blossoming inherent value.
They never have
and they never, ever, will.

If you're struggling, please reach out ; (Further resources listed on pg. 258)

Sick Days

(Mild Trigger Warning: Trichotillomania)

I hope you know your hair doesn't define you.
But even if it did, I'd still think you were beautiful
because it's unique and kinda cool and you pull it off
better than I ever could.

I hope you know that wig / hat / scarf
looks absolutely perfect on you.
You look like the kind of person
I'd stare at on the sidewalk
wondering how it feels to look that *cool*.

I also hope you know you'd look just as amazing without it.

I hope you know that
what I am really trying to say is
that nobody else is as worried about
or critical of
your looks
as you think they are
but that even if they were
they would have nothing honest to say
except that you're
glowing.

Crisis Textline ; *CrisisTextline.org* ; Text # 741741 (in US and Canada)

Chloe Alessandra Henkel

My favorite photo of myself
is from when I was four-years-old and fearless.
I am wearing a canary yellow dress
and smiling at someone off-camera
while stepping forward with my arms out,
ready to embrace anything.
I want to live up to the version of myself
that I was
back then.
I am determined to be
unafraid and bursting with smiles again.

If you're struggling, please reach out ; (Further resources listed on pg. 258)

Sick Days

Just because you don't have a family
right this moment
doesn't mean you never will.
Someday, you'll be a part of somebody's
lost-and-found family.
You'll be the one with the shoulder they cry on
and the one whose number they all have on speed-dial
to call the second that they get
the best or the worst of news.
You'll have your own little group of friends
who know (and love)
all those weird, quirky, things about you
and they'll all fall short
whenever they're asked to describe you
because they won't know how to put into words
all the simple, perfect, ways that you are.
They'll go to concerts with you
(even if they don't all love the same music as you do)
because they know how happy it makes you.
At the end of the day,
you are going to matter so much to them
that they would do anything to make you happy,
when really,
knowing that
will be more than enough
to do just that.

Crisis Textline ; *CrisisTextline.org* ; Text # 741741 (in US and Canada)
Chloe Alessandra Henkel

A few of the things I want for you:

The realization that a lot of things won't go as planned, and that it's possible to be okay with that.

The ability to calm your own inner-storms: to change what you can't accept and accept what you can't change, for lack of a better cliché.

The feeling that comes with really knowing that no matter how low things get, they'll get better again. You'll be okay in the end. You have a beautiful life still ahead of you.

Good food, and movies that are so bad they're funny.

Fun, weird, wild, annual traditions with your friends.

A favorite store, a favorite show, a favorite place to go.

The self-love that it takes to really heal your own wounds.

Someone(s) who love you so much it feels like the two of you are cut from the same piece of cloth. Like you're not just an open book, but two halves of the same one.

The realization that you matter. And that you don't deserve to blame yourself for every little thing that goes awry.

A home with a yard full of grass so green it's almost blinding, with a picture-perfect sky to match.

All or none of these things, in whatever amounts you need to be where you want to be.

Healing.

If you're struggling, please reach out ; (Further resources listed on pg. 258)

Sick Days

Someday, it'll be summer again
and we'll be driving down back roads in my car
with the windows down,
the cool breeze splashing us like water balloons.
You'll be happy and I'll be happy
and this sadness and hurt will feel like a distant memory.

We'll be a little bit older and a whole lot wiser
and we'll have jobs that we like
more than we thought we would
and even if things aren't perfect
they'll be so much better than we thought they'd be
and that'll be enough to make it feel perfect to us.

My point is that all of this is going to pass
and turn into something else.
You'll have regrets and you'll have proudest moments
but you'll learn not to let any of it break you.

Someday, you'll be so happy to be here.

Crisis Textline ; *CrisisTextline.org* ; Text # 741741 (in US and Canada)

Chloe Alessandra Henkel

We had a party! in the kitchen today
with wine glasses and sweets and everything.

Of course, it was quick *(speed round! musical chairs!)*
because I had schoolwork and my brother had schoolwork
and my father had work and my mother had taxes to file
but we had to eat lunch sometime and when we ate lunch
We decided
we'd make it a party.

So we had cookies and
shot glasses of
bubbly soda
with which we made a toast
to our party!
and drank up.

Because why sit around waiting
for something to smile about
when we can make it ourselves?

(You can join in our party, too.
You can eat a cookie
sip a drink
or just spend a minute
dancing in the kitchen too
if you want to).

If you're struggling, please reach out ; (Further resources listed on pg. 258)

Sick Days

The thing they don't tell you
about being forced to make flint-and-steel fires
to burn your way out of
black-ink-nights
is that it can become a power all its own.
By learning and re-learning
all the ways to (and not to) dissolve the walls
around yourself
you've inadvertently written maps
in your palms
of all the places you've been
and gained the power to heal
anyone uncertain
of the cluttered path on which
you've already travelled this far.

Crisis Textline ; *CrisisTextline.org* ; Text # 741741 (in US and Canada)

Chloe Alessandra Henkel

I am actually
perfectly
gorgeous.

The thought leaves me breathless
but rings true
nonetheless.

Loving my life
and jumping into it
without regrets;
it's such a strange feeling
and I'm drunk on it.

It is golden outside
and I am
so lucky
to be alive.

Even if I never have another thing
to be grateful for
this
would still be more than enough
to make everything else worthwhile.

If you're struggling, please reach out ; (Further resources listed on pg. 258)

Sick Days

A Letter To Myself (written June 4th, 2020 – two weeks after my high school graduation day)

Dear me, 9 months ago,
I know you're struggling.
I know you're depressed.
I know you just left public school
because of it.
I know you don't even think you'll graduate.
Little do you know, you will—
                                       — a year early.
You'll publish that book you wrote before you do
and get your driver's license a week after.
You'll still have hard days
but you learn to be okay with that.
So just hang in there until then, okay?

Crisis Textline ; *CrisisTextline.org* ; Text # 741741 (in US and Canada)
Chloe Alessandra Henkel

I have always been flooded with *why why why*'s.

Why am I the way I am?
Why am I always imploding like this?
Why doesn't he like me?
Why doesn't anything I see make sense to me?
Why is it so hard to talk to people?
Why are there so many questions and so few answers?

But the truth is
some questions don't need answers: just time.

If you're struggling, please reach out ; (Further resources listed on pg. 258)

Sick Days

I've thought about it a lot:
wondering if I would change it, if I could.
Wondering if, given a magic wand and the option
I would undo
everything I went through
to get where I am.
And I don't think I would.

I wouldn't wish the hard parts on anybody
(although I know everybody has their own
regardless)
and I am doing my best to change it
(change the negative thoughts,
change the storm-drain feelings)
for the future.

But all of the places I've been
have helped make me who I am.
I don't know the person I would be without them,
and I'm finally happy
with the person I am.

Chloe Alessandra Henkel

I'm not going to pretend to have all of the answers.
Or even half of the answers.
I don't.
But I really, really care about you.
And I honestly, truly, believe
that no matter how terrible things may be
you are going to make it through them.
Call it experience, call it intuition,
call it whatever you want to:
the fact is, I have faith in you.
I think you were given this life for a reason.
And that even if there isn't a reason
for the lives each one of us has been tossed into
that we can give them one ourselves.
We are the captains of our own ships
and we have the power to make them
incredible.
And I know
one way or another
that you
and your butterfly fingers
(beautiful, delicate, brimming with questions)
are only just beginning.
I know that you
are in the process of growing
into
even more than the person
you'd hoped to be.
I don't have all the answers
but the one I have, I'm certain of:
*you deserve the world
and you'll have it one day.*

If you're struggling, please reach out ; (Further resources listed on pg. 258)

Sick Days

(Trigger Warning: Trichotillomania)

Friends and strangers used to call me *Rapunzel,*
as in, *Rapunzel, Rapunzel, let down your long hair!*
as in, golden locks of fairytales.

I guess they forgot how Rapunzel's story ended,
or how that 'ending' was just the beginning
of the rest of her life,
beyond the tower she'd been locked away in.

She was freer without the hair.

Chloe Alessandra Henkel

I fall in love with stop signs and rain and songs on the radio. I fall in love with thrift stores and the ways strangers tie their shoes and a quickly growing multitude of things. I throw love like confetti, leaving it everywhere, even the places I'm not anymore. I can't stand the idea that there's such a thing as craving love too strongly, or loving too much. Too easily. Too openly. Because this love-filled heart of mine is too big and too pellucid to be anything but an open book.

If you're struggling, please reach out ; (Further resources listed on pg. 258)

Sick Days

Did you love yourself today?
And before you answer: I'm not just asking if
the two of you coexisted, warless.

I'm asking if you took the time to brush your hair
and braid it,
just the way you like.

If you put a little extra jam on your morning bagel,
but made sure to take your vitamins with it.

If you soothed yourself
with gentle hugs and words made of honeysuckle
(it's okay, darling)
when you started to tense

and if, when that person you've been loving from afar
glanced over
you told yourself "it's okay, just smile!"
instead of
"they're probably staring at that girl to the right."

I'm asking if you called yourself *stunning*
and tucked yourself in nicely
at night.

So I'll ask you again, one more time, think it over:
did you love yourself today?

Crisis Textline ; *CrisisTextline.org* ; Text # 741741 (in US and Canada)

Chloe Alessandra Henkel

I don't wear my favorite shirt as much as I should.
I look at it and smile
almost pick it up
then put it back down
far too often.
I worry that it'll get worn (out)
or ripped
or scuffed up
if I wear it too much
or I that I won't get it in the laundry in time
for the next time
I *reeeeeally* need to wear it
or I worry about a million other things
for a million other reasons
and I let each one
make the decision for me
and so
I hardly wear it at all.
And it's taken me this long
to realize
I'm doing things all wrong.
I should be wearing that sweet, comfy, shirt with the stripes
every single day that I'm alive and able!
I'm putting it on right now
and not taking it off
until its torn at every seam,
and even then
I'll pull out my sewing kit
stitch it up
and pull it back on
all over again.

If you're struggling, please reach out ; (Further resources listed on pg. 258)

Sick Days

Fuck it. Let's hold hands like we mean it, locking our fingers together for good. Let's watch the sunset on picnics, and hold hands in abandoned buildings. You can watch me skin my knees at the skate park, and we'll buy slushies with crumpled dollar bills afterwards. Let's sing sad songs at the top of our lungs with the windows down, laughing until we cry or crying until we laugh, whichever one seems more right when we get there. Let's leave notes for strangers on public benches and color our hair with discount box dye. Let's stay up all night watching cheaply made horror movies. Let's enjoy all of the pointless, meaningful, things this life has to offer; together.

Crisis Textline ; *CrisisTextline.org* ; Text # 741741 (in US and Canada)

Chloe Alessandra Henkel

I refuse to waste my life being afraid
whenever I can help it.

I'm going skinny dipping without wondering
who's watching
because how many times in a lifetime do you get the chance
to do something as thrilling as this?

Who cares what anybody else thinks of me
as long as I'm myself and I'm happy?
I'm hugging myself and loving every piece of her.
I'm borrowing confidence from the stars
and wearing it like a second skin.

And, along with it, I'm wearing
whatever wild, crazy, clothing I like best
without choking up wondering what other people think of it.

I'm reveling in all the second glances I get
instead of mentally reminding myself to *quiet down*.
I'm no longer afraid to be loud.

If you're struggling, please reach out ; (Further resources listed on pg. 258)

Sick Days

Today, I found the sun and climbed
high enough to touch it
ignoring the whispers of the passerby below.
I walked past a pasture of cows and stood outside the fence
mooing back at them and laughing until my stomach hurt.
I picked a bundle of flowers to dry and press
because sometimes beautiful things
can be made permanent.
I let handfuls of chocolate melt on my tongue
while watching clouds foam and tumble
across the skyline.
There is mud all over the soles of my shoes
and chunks of grass and sky under my fingernails.
I wouldn't have it any other way.

Crisis Textline ; *CrisisTextline.org* ; Text # 741741 (in US and Canada)
Chloe Alessandra Henkel

One of the best feelings I've ever had
is the feeling of being able to help someone
who is where I am
or where I was.

One of the best feelings I've ever had
is throwing someone a hotline
or a therapist's number
that they ended up using, or
walking hand-in-hand with someone
to their first appointment
after telling them all about mine
and how it wasn't nearly as scary
as it seemed like it would be.

One of the best feelings I've ever had
being able to be somebody's band-aid
and finding a practical purpose for all of my
bittersweet empathy
and the turmoil
around and within me.

One of the best feelings I've ever had
is picking up my broken glass pieces
and making myself
a sun-catcher.

If you're struggling, please reach out ; (Further resources listed on pg. 258)

Sick Days

Living in this generation, in this time, in the world as we know it is hard. It's scary. It's chaotic. But it's also amazing. Because we are making it amazing. Because when we see things wrong in the world, we are speaking up and changing them. We are choosing to reconnect with the world around us. We are bringing back red lipstick smiles and candid photographs. We're learning to love life through supermarket photoshoots and parking lot strolls with friends. We are using networking to help each other like never before. And we have amazing things, like cotton candy. Travelling fairs in the summertime. Gadgets that can play any song in the world, out loud, on cue. We still have a chance at saving our blue skies and lush trees. We still have post offices and stamps and envelopes and letters to be written and poems to be read and skirts to be sewn. We have jokes, jokes which can stay between two friends, or be shared with hundreds of millions of people in minutes. We still live in a world with songbirds and bullfrogs, all of which sing, sing for you, if you're listening. We have funnel cake and the oldest family recipes in history. We have food trucks that taste like paradise, little pockets of bliss scattered across street corners. We have old book stores cluttered with hardbacks watched over by bookstore cats. We have lemon water, and cars that don't eat gasoline. We have more words in the dictionary than ever before. We have safe spaces and invisible braces. We have mail-order butterflies.

What I mean to say is that, in spite of everything, there is still so much good to be found about the here and now.

Crisis Textline ; *CrisisTextline.org* ; Text # 741741 (in US and Canada)

Chloe Alessandra Henkel

Raging storms
rattle your hands
from the inside
but you tame them with the force
of a gentle breeze.

Hurricanes shake the storm shutters
of your knees
until you think they may buckle
but you handle them better
than the universe itself
imagined you would.

You are so strong
and you don't even know it yet.

You are the antithesis of weakness.

If you're struggling, please reach out ; (Further resources listed on pg. 258)

Sick Days

I'm so proud of you.
Please keep holding on.
That's all you need to do for now:
Hold on. Be here.
Everything else can come later.

Crisis Textline ; *CrisisTextline.org* ; Text # 741741 (in US and Canada)

Chloe Alessandra Henkel

On one hand,
I am a collector of acorns and sharks' teeth:
a pair of hands that knows how to find things.

On the other hand,
I am the girl who can't read a map for the life of her:
a mind that knows loss like that back of its hand.

Only now,
I am learning how to put these hands together
because one side of me
need not
outweigh the other:
I am a messy whole
made of seashells and road signs
made of apple juice and dog bites
made of butterfly wings and lost & found things.

In both hands,
I am a work-in-progress
who is nothing short of a miracle.
I am the universe's way of sticking it to the odds
and I am determined
to exist
in spite of all the unsteadiness
that comes with this,
this way that I hold
what could be considered
everything.

If you're struggling, please reach out ; (Further resources listed on pg. 258)

Sick Days

I want to take you one more place:
our final stop for the day.
You can open your eyes, we're here!

The ocean was the first place I felt
wholly, completely, unafraid.
Something about staring up
at sun-speckled clouds
with nothing but rumbling saltwater
separating me from sand and sky
makes me feel infinite and free.

I wanted to bottle this feeling
and leave it on your doorstep
but since I haven't figured out how to do that yet
I decided to bring you here instead.

You deserve this feeling a million times over.

Crisis Textline ; *CrisisTextline.org* ; Text # 741741 (in US and Canada)

Chloe Alessandra Henkel

I am irrevocably glad to be alive.
I am scarred and serendipitous and perfect and in love with
everything and everyone I know.
I am running through thrift stores
wearing an old wedding gown and no shoes.
I am cinnamon sugar toast, sweet butter on bread.
I am shouting into the wind and bursting out laughing,
laughing until I cry, but the crying is the happy kind.
I give and receive kisses on cheeks in warm rain.
I am learning to hug, to hold, to keep again.
I scribble messy sketches and pin them to my wall with pride.
I am not afraid to write entire poems on loving myself.
I am a fortune cookie with buttercup blooms inside.
I stand on stages after-hours and sing my heart out
for me, and me alone
delighting in the way my words ricochet off the ceiling.
I am beat-up sneakers and grass-stained jeans.
I am a stargazer with newfound patience.
I am happy, unabashedly.
I could not be more grateful to have survived
everything that I thought would be the end of me.
And no matter where you are now,
I promise you'll get here too, with time.

(NOT) THE END

If you're struggling, please reach out ; (Further resources listed on pg. 258)

Sick Days

It's okay if you didn't find all of yourself, or exactly what
you needed. between these pages. As much as I hope you
did, I'm guessing that not everybody will, and that's *okay*.
You're still valid. You're still going to be okay.
And you know what?
That's part of why I wrote this book.
Because as much as I searched, there were certain parts of
me I couldn't find out in the world.
So, I decided to be the one to write them.
Whether this book is or isn't a place of hope for you,
your places and your people are out there.
You'll find them, you'll build them,
you'll figure things out and find your place,
in time.
In the meantime,
you can stay as long as you need
in mine.

Resources

I also want you to have these. Please use them as much as you need them. They're here for you, and you deserve all the help you need and then some.

If you're struggling, reach out.

I love you and that beautiful soul of yours too much to imagine you struggling alone.

*** If you don't know where to start: check out *www.CrisisTextLine.org* – they're available to help with any kind of crisis, no matter how big or small. ***

Please Note: These resources are, to my knowledge, accurate and up-to-date as of the publication of this book. For the most up-to-date information, please check in with your local healthcare providers, government resources, and other local mental health resources.

And please <u>call emergency services (911 if in the U.S.) if you, or anyone you know, are in immediate danger</u>.

<u>The Crisis Textline;</u> *www.CrisisTextline.org*
Textline Number: 741741 if in U.S. or Canada
                        85258 if in the U.K.
                        50808 if in Ireland

<u>National Domestic Violence Hotline;</u> *www.TheHotline.org*
Hotline Number: 800-799-7233 (if in the U.S.)

(continued on next page)

If you're struggling, please reach out ; (Further resources listed on pg. 258)

Sick Days

National Suicide Prevention Lifeline;
www.SuicidePreventionLifeline.org
Lifeline Number: 1-800-273-8255 (if in the U.S.)

RAINN (The Rape, Abuse & Incest National Network);
www.RAINN.org
National Sexual Assault Telephone Hotline Number:
800-656-4673 (if in the U.S.)

Samaritans (European Mental Health / Emotional Support Resource); *www.samaritans.org*
Phone Number: 116 123 (if in the U.K.)
Email: jo@samaritans.org

SAMHSA (Substance Abuse and Mental Health Services Administration); *www.SAMHSA.gov*
Helpline Number (offering referrals to treatment and support, and resources for addiction, substance abuse, and mental health issues): 1-800-662-4357 (if in the U.S.)

Stand With Trans (a resource for Transgender individuals, and parents of Transgender individuals);
www.StandWithTrans.org

The TLC Foundation for BFRBs (a resource for learning more about Trichotillomania and other Body-Focused Repetitive Behaviors); *www.BFRB.org*

The Loveland Foundation (a resource that provides financial assistance to cover therapy costs for black women and girls) *www.TheLoveLandFoundation.org*

(continued on next page)

Crisis Textline ; *CrisisTextline.org* ; Text # 741741 (in US and Canada)

Chloe Alessandra Henkel

Therapy For Black Girls (an online mental health space/resource for black girls/women);
www.TherapyForBlackGirls.com

Trans Lifeline (a resource for Transgender individuals);
www.TransLifeline.org
Lifeline Number: 877-565-8860 (if in the U.S.)
                 877-330-6366 (if in Canada)

The Trevor Project (a LGBTQ+ mental health resource);
www.TheTrevorProject.org
Lifeline Number: 1-866-488-7386 (if in the U.S.)
TrevorText Textline Number: 678-678 (if in the U.S.)

***Also Note:* Many resources offer online chat features, and other resources on their websites, so even if the above Textline/Lifeline numbers aren't available where you are, you may still be able to receive help by visiting the websites listed. Please stay safe and take care!**

Want to reach out (to a resource here, or a counsellor, friend/family member, etc. but don't know what to say?

Start with: "I'm really struggling/anxious/sad right now and I'm not sure what to do. Can you help me through it?" and go from there.

If you're struggling, please reach out ; (Further resources listed on pg. 258)

Sick Days

Things to Do When Struggling

Here are just some general ideas of things to do when you're struggling (whether you're sad, anxious, overthinking, or anything else)

-Take a few deeeeeep, steady, breaths

-Try the five senses grounding exercise;

(grounding yourself by listing things that you can see, hear, taste, smell, and touch—or, if you don't have all of those things at the moment, list things you *like to* see, hear, taste, smell, and touch)

-Read a book, or re-read your favorite pages in this book

-Listen to music

-Sing, or play an instrument (I personally love the ukulele)

-Watch a movie or TV show

-Drink some hot tea or hot chocolate

-Draw, paint, or make a collage

-Draw or paint on yourself with skin-safe paint/pens

-Write. Whether it's writing a poem/story, or just journaling whatever words come to mind and venting, I find this one to be infinitely helpful.

-Clean your room or workspace, one item at a time, until it's all tidied up.

Chloe Alessandra Henkel

-Make a list of all of the positive things about you, or things you've accomplished (keep this list and add to it whenever possible. look over it when in need of a boost)

-Make a list of your favorite things. If you don't know where to start, start with your favorite...
animal, plant, band, song (at the moment), shirt, book, food, dessert, holiday, season, restaurant, store, etc.

-Go outside and spend one whole minute doing nothing.

-Spend time with a pet

-Go for a walk

-Squeeze a stress ball or hold onto an ice cube

-Try using some essential oils or nice perfume

-Write a letter to someone else, or your future/past self

-Make a list of future goals

-Try a new hobby. Sewing, making jewelry, going to the gym, growing plants, anything

-Squeeze a pillow or snap a rubber band against your arm

-Comb/brush your hair

-Play with fidget toys

-Compliment two people (friends or strangers)

-Go thrifting/shopping

If you're struggling, please reach out ; (Further resources listed on pg. 258)

Sick Days

Ducky (aka Samson) & Harry for sitting with me while I wrote this book, and for making me smile daily.

Everyone in my Group Therapy, and all the other people (friends, family, or strangers) who have shared their stories with me: For making me feel so much less alone, and for trusting me with such big pieces of you.

For everyone who I'm going to meet someday: for existing. For being out there and giving me a little extra hope in the future. *I can't wait to meet you.*

You, my beautiful family of fireflies: For being here. For being yourselves, for existing. And for continuing to glow, no matter how dark things get. No matter how you ended up here, with this book in your hands, with your eyes on this page, I'm glad you did. I value you so much more than you know. I think of all of you often. I hope you're happy, hope you're well. I hope I've managed to give you something. I can't even seem to find the words to tell you what you mean to me. The closest I can come is *'nearly everything.'*

Please remember that no matter how hard things may feel at times, you are absolutely never alone. You are necessary, and so worthy of care. Things will get better.

I love you, always.

About the Author

Chloe Alessandra Henkel is 18 years old (as of the writing of this book). Born in West Virginia and raised in Maryland, she is a poet, author, artist, and college student.

She has written, edited, and designed a number of books, and has been featured in *To Write Love on Her Arms, Gurls Talk, Our Minds* and other publications.

When not reading or writing, she can probably be found with her friends, pets, or boyfriend, thrifting, going on long walks with her family, or rambling to her therapist.

For more, follow her
Instagram: @chloe.creating
TikTok: @chloe.creating
YouTube: Chloe Creating

Made in the USA
Monee, IL
29 March 2022